Call Me If You Have Questions

Laura de Blank

Cover art: *Baie St. Paul*, oil on canvas, 1942, by Jack Lowrey

DEDICATION

To Paul, for encouraging me in all things. Thank you for finding my stories interesting, and telling me to write them down.

To my children, children-in-law, and grandchildren, for making my life rich and satisfying.

To my distant descendants, for reading this book.

ACKNOWLEDGMENTS

I want to thank Elizabeth McNeil, my teacher, my editor, my friend.

Why I Wrote This and Why You Should Read It

I am descended from a long line of people who have written down their every thought and never thrown away so much as a scrap of paper. I know this because in June 2016, I was given all the family papers—fourteen moldy boxes and a damp trunk. The papers used to live in my uncle Henry's attic. He and my mother were the family historians, so this arrangement was deemed proper and didn't inconvenience any of the rest of us. If anyone had a question about family history, you just asked Uncle Henry or my mother, and they would answer it.

When Uncle Henry died, and the old house was sold, the papers went to his son Dan's basement. My cousin Dan always said he was interested in family history, but I'm not sure he got around to reading those papers before he, too, died. Dan's widow Wendy wanted the papers out of her basement, so she notified all members of the family, and over the next year or two, each person came to Wendy's basement, looked at the mountain of boxes, and despaired. A few of them took away a photo or two, just to be a good sport, but no one wanted all of it.

I was not interested enough in the family history even to show up at Wendy's house, and my silence was therefore taken as consent. Wendy lives in Rockport, Massachusetts, and I live in Hyannis Port, Massachusetts, during the summers, in the house I inherited from my parents. Geographically, the decision of what to do with the papers was a simple one. My cousin Nina called one morning and announced that she and her husband John were on their way with the fourteen boxes and the trunk. I could do whatever I wanted with them.

I stacked the boxes in a teetering mountain along two walls of the dining room and sat down at the table to read. I naively assumed that I would be able to discard all the uninteresting bits and reduce the mountain to one or two small boxes. If, indeed, there was anything of interest in there at all.

The boxes held a great many unidentified photographs of bewhiskered old men and small round babies wearing frilly dresses and weasel-skin caps. There's no pretending I wasn't alarmed and somewhat despondent, not about the caps, but about the amount of work to do. But, on the other hand, it was also fascinating. Surely somewhere in one of these boxes would be another photograph of that old man and the baby that would be labeled, and I could solve those small mysteries.

So I sat at the breakfast table for hours each morning, and kept reading throughout the summer. Ledgers accounted for the cost of nails and barrel hoops in 1784. Brochures advertised my grandfather's prefabricated workman's village in the 1930s. Newspaper articles from the 1940s praised my grandmother's work for the American Society for Psychical Research. A handwritten story described a maiden friend of the family rescuing the household goods from the marauding Hessian mercenaries during the American Revolution. Another described my great-great-grandfather getting a safe pass to reclaim the body of his son, Thomas Haines, from his battlefield grave during the Civil War.

Nearly indecipherable letters tell of life in London during World War I, and others of the bombs falling from World War II's Battle of Britain, fought high above Devon. The letters stop abruptly in mid-1940. However, that village of voices—Aunt Julie, Aunt Lottie, the four generations of Grosvenors, Uncle Royal, Grace, Jack, Gordon, Kate, and Virnie—kept me awake at night as they continued their conversations in my head.

I soon realized that if no one before me had thrown out these papers, then I couldn't do it either. Online, I ordered archival files, tissue paper, polyester sleeves, and boxes. As I read the papers, I worked to organize and conserve them. Someday, when one of you, my descendants, wants to do your PhD dissertation on early American history, remember that the primary source material is in the cupboard under the stairs at Hyannis Port.

As for the memories that follow here, I began writing them long before I received the family papers. But it was only after I spent a summer reading about the family's lives that I knew why I was writing my own.

It is some sort of biological imperative, and I can't help myself.

The family began saving their papers about 1780, with letters from the brothers Jeremiah, Josiah, and Isaac Pierson, about building their iron manufacturing company in Ramapo, New York. The papers continue until 1940, and I was born in 1946. My memories continue the family narrative for the next seventy years, bringing us to 2017.

If you allow my memories to age gracefully in the cupboard under the stairs for a hundred years, they will become fascinating, too. And mine are legible.

Call Me If You Have Questions

Part I

Some Family History

Family Secrets

My family has had their share of failures and triumphs. Their stories are not secret, unless they become forgotten.

The stories I know come from my mother's side of my family, because she was a teller of true tales. My father was a teller of imaginary ones. He told us how he had been a scout for the Blackfoot Indians when he was a small child, showing us photos of himself in his sailor suit and straw boater hat as proof, asking us, in all seriousness, if we thought he would ever wear those clothes if they weren't necessary as a clever disguise. But he didn't tell us real stories. The only stories I know of his family are the ones our mother told us.

Mother's stories always had a moral—they were teaching stories. She knew lots of girls who had died, at just the ages of my sister and myself, of everything we wanted to do. There was the girl who choked on a cherry pit because she was running while eating; the girl who died of starvation because she was such a picky eater; and most curious of all was the girl who died of a bad oyster because she was too polite to spit it out.

Not to be outdone in parental fear, my father told us an improving tale about the little boy who died ice skating because when he fell down he just lay there, admiring the clouds drifting by, and another boy skated up and accidently sliced his wrist with his skate blade.

My parents had a cautionary tale for every possible way to die.

As we grew older, Mother's stories changed from how to avoid death to how to live. They hinted at the dramatic adult world waiting in our future—a world with rules that were different from those we children played by, and with stakes that were far higher.

Mother's tales began in May of 1862, when my great-grandmother, Laura Tryon, married my great-grandfather, Grosvenor Lowrey, who was Edison's patent lawyer. I know the date because I wear her wedding ring on my little finger, and the date is engraved inside, along with their initials. They lived in Tarrytown, New York. Laura had five children in eleven years, and then died of cancer in 1879.

The children, Frank, Royal, Grovie, Virginia (my grandmother), and Julie, were young, and their father needed help. He had a steamy romance with Kate Armour, a young Canadian woman half his age, and married her in 1880. They had two more children: Grace and Jack. Kate was a good stepmother for many years, but after her husband Grosvenor died in 1893, she wanted all these stepchildren safely settled so she could move on with her life. She married Virginia off to the first man who proposed to her: Frank Ball.

However, according to my side of the family, Frank was a thorough, no-good rotter.

Frank lived and worked in the American community in Kobe, Japan, and took Virginia back there with him in 1895, when she was twenty-two. He left her alone in the house while he spent time with his Japanese wife and children across town. Apparently, he also slept with every other woman he could find. In the stories handed down from my mother, Frank was also an alcoholic and a wife beater.

Virginia was miserable and stuck. She had no money of her own, her father had died, and her stepmother Kate had remarried a Canadian named Hayter Reed. Kate, Grace, and Jack had moved to Ottawa, and Kate had another child: Gordon Reed.

Virginia and Frank Ball had two sons: Grosvenor and Penn. Virginia struggled along for many years in Japan, and then her young son, Penn, died of scarlet fever. Now Virginia had only one son to protect, six-year-old Grosvenor, and one less reason to stay with Frank Ball. So she packed up Grosvenor, and with her small savings started east around the world to get home to the United States. She stretched her money out by stopping with friends and acquaintances whenever she could, and stayed with a school friend in Paris long enough to find work in a milliner's shop, earning the rest of the money for the transatlantic fare.

Meanwhile, most of her siblings also struggled. Grosvenor was a doctor who became addicted to his own prescriptions. The family sent him to live quietly in Ireland. After Frank went to South America to become a cowboy on the pampas, Royal was dispatched to find him and bring him home. Their sister Julie married an Englishman named Herbert Baggallay, and was happy. Their half-brother, Jack, although an alcoholic, became an excellent artist. I have three of his paintings. He married a Russian ballerina, named Olga, but the marriage lasted only three weeks.

Jack's brief marriage was one of those stories for which my mother's only response to our questions was to raise her eyebrows. They were very expressive eyebrows. They silently signaled that there was a story there if only she would tell it. But she never did.

Jack's sister, Grace Lowrey, married a man named Howard Daly, who went down with the Lusitania in 1915, but popped up again and was rescued. Grace battled depression all her life and ultimately killed herself. The family said that Howard married his mistress on the day of Grace's funeral.

One morning over breakfast, when mother was in a storytelling mood, she told my sister and me that when she was a teenager, she was assigned the job of escorting the then adult Grace home to Ottawa, after her visit to the family in New York. Grace was deemed too depressed to travel alone. Mother said she was terrified by the responsibility and didn't let Grace go to the bathroom alone for the two days of their trip.

In her forties, Grace moved in with her younger half-brother Gordon. A few years later, Gordon and his fiancée Marian returned after a walk in the autumn woods, calling out to Grace to tell her they were home. They got no response. The situation had gotten so bad that they immediately assumed she had killed herself. To spare Gordon from having to see whatever had happened, Marian told him to wait downstairs while she went up to look. Grace had shot herself.

Virginia eventually got herself back to New York and settled down with her son Grosvenor. Her stepmother, Kate Lowrey Reed, helped her get a divorce from Frank Ball, saying, "I got you into this mess. The least I can do is to get you out of it."

As a divorced woman, Virginia assumed no one would ever want to marry her, but my grandfather, Tom Pierson, did. He didn't seem to notice or care that she was no longer young, idealistic, and virginal. They had two more children: my uncle Henry and my mother Jocelyn. The span between Virginia's surviving children was almost twenty years. Jocelyn was a flower girl at Grosvenor's wedding. My grandmother wrote a semi-autobiographical novel about this time in her life, titled *Via the P & O*, under the pen name Jane Stocking.

*   *   *   *

My mother gave us glimpses of the adult world through the stories of her family. She honored the people who lived these stories by not forgetting them. She seemed, in addition, to have an ambivalent attitude toward errors. She didn't want us to die young of avoidable stupidities; she wanted us to learn from the past, take some risks, make our own mistakes.

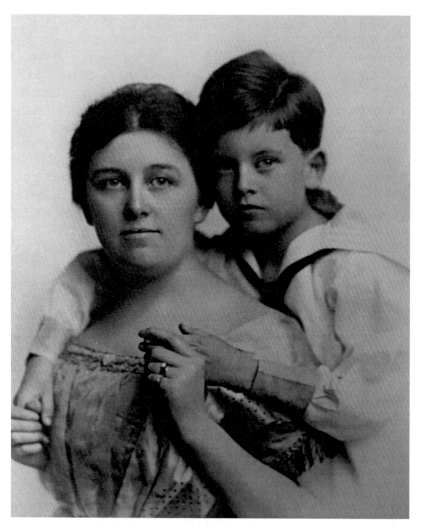

My father Richard L. Kennedy, Jr., and his mother Jane McLeod Kennedy, 1910

Granite Love

Affectionately posed, my father leans over
His mother's shoulder, cheek pressed
Against her hair, his hands reaching
Around to hold hers.

Two generations with the same dark hair,
Blue eyes.
She in a dress of silk with tucks of tiny stitches,
He in his sailor suit,
They wear their best for this moment of immortality.

Mother and son look directly at me.
Her face is calm.
His eyes serious,
His arms protect her.
They lean together.

The father,
The missing "um" of this triumvirate,
Would look normal on the outside, black suit, white shirt.
Within, he is a swirling storm,
Lawyer for the railroad, successful
Against its widows and its orphans.

At Christmas he gives his son a hockey jersey.
The boy wonders, will it have the player number of a legend—
St. Paul's Tony Conroy or Moose Goheen?
He unfolds the shirt and holds it up to show
On its back the number "zero."

"That's how you skate," the father says to his son's averted face,
Then looks around the room for others to enjoy his joke.
What does the mother say to that?
Alone at bedtime, they lean together:
"You're not a zero," she whispers.

"He sees you only through the filter
Of his misery. Bear with him."

I see myself in their eyes, their hair,
But not in their granite love.
All their lives they lean together
To carry the weight of that sorry
Son of a Bitch.

It's So Damn Hard to Be Fair

My mother, born and bred in the north, conceded that, although the institution of American slavery had not been a good thing overall, the Black people enslaved by it were, in general, a happy group.

"Unhappiness," she told me, "is caused by the fear of losing your property or wealth, or the actual loss of those things, and since the slaves had no wealth, they were happy."

I just looked at her.

My mother, a grande dame who resembled Joan Crawford, told me many things that amazed me. She lived in a different world than I did. One evening when she came upon me curled up on the sofa scaring myself with Tolkien's *The Lord of the Rings*, she looked at me briefly, before passing through the room, and said, "I don't read fiction. I have a very good imagination and can tell myself stories."

This maxim reverberated through our family with variations depending on the situation. "No, thank you," my sister said, "I don't want to attend the symphony. I can whistle."

My mother was a woman of unflagging energy and unfathomable opinions. To me, she seemed larger than life.

My children, who knew Mother well only after she moved to Phoenix in her old age, might have said she was ferocious, biased, politically so incorrect as to be off the scale, tactless, grumpy, and proud of them.

Peeling back the layers, I remember Mother when she was younger, and was my mother instead of my responsibility. And going back another layer, I also remember the stories she told me of her own youth, when she was simply a young woman.

In her twenties, Mother worked as an investigator for the Society of Psychical Research in New York. She was sent out in response to calls reporting small poltergeist manifestations or full-scale hauntings.

Once, she went with her cousin Lydia in response to a call involving a mysterious light that danced around the front hall of an old apartment building. Whenever the light danced, the residents reported feeling a cold breeze, and a chill went down their spines. Mother and Lydia looked the hallway over and asked for a broom.

Turning off the lights, with all the residents seated on the stairs watching them, they waited for the dancing light to appear. Sure enough, there it was. "See, see!" the residents yelled, exulting in the compliant appearance of their ghost. Mother and Lydia attacked the light with the broom, chasing it from one wall to the next. Eventually, winded, they turned the lights back on and sat down on the stairs with the others to think.

"What is upstairs?" Mother asked.

"Just a hallway like this one with more apartments on either side."

"Let me see it," Mother said, grasping her broom tightly.

The dusty flight of stairs led to another hallway, dimly lit by a bulb hanging from the ceiling by a long cord, which swayed slightly as a summer breeze from the open window blew the light curtains.

Mother and Lydia trooped back downstairs, knowing now what they were looking for: a hole the size of a pin that would permit the upstairs light to enter the downstairs hall, and they found it.

Mother never investigated a claim of the supernatural that she couldn't explain away naturally, but that didn't lessen the ferocity of her belief in the existence of otherworldly life.

I went to a psychic reading with Mother once in London. We stopped at a stationer's, where she bought a yellow pad and a pen. She told me to write down every word that anyone said during the séance. "A medium will often get you talking and then amaze you with details of your life that she deduces from your own conversation, not from the spirits at all. So it's vital to remember what you've told her."

The medium was a comfortable middle-aged woman with tightly curled gray hair and a bright smile that seemed forced. We sat in the living room of her apartment, a cozy room with chintz-covered armchairs and plastic daffodils in the windowsill. It was the opposite of the movie version of a dark, possibly foggy place to contact the dead.

Quite understandably, the medium frowned at my notetaking and said, "I feeeeel the presence of an Unbeliever. Let us hooooope that this negative energy doesn't discourage the spirits." She glared at me.

I wanted to deny it. My mother is making me take these notes, I wanted to say. She is the skeptic, not I. But come to think of it, why can't your spirit guides tell you which of us wants detailed notes?

Later, among my mother's papers, I found the notes from that meeting, carefully transcribed by her. The medium talked a lot, and Mother found meaning in much of it. The medium saw a vision of blue and white Delft tiles, and although Mother would have been silent at the time, in the typed transcript of this meeting, she comments that this must be a reference to my husband Paul who is half Dutch and was raised in Holland. The medium saw a brown, curly animal, and Mother's typed comment was that this probably referred to my dog Brownie.

I admire my mother's desire to meet a struggling medium halfway, but she never answered my question of why the spirits would take time out of their busy celestial routines to tell us vague things we already knew.

My mother had as many facets as a diamond. As a young woman, she was invited to a party on Howard Hughes's yacht. When he said goodbye to her at the gangplank, he asked for her telephone number. My mother might have been a snob, but she wasn't a social climber. She truly believed that being descended from people who fought in the American Revolution made her more important than people who weren't. Her insecurities arose from a concern that other people might not know the details of her lineage. In her opinion, she was already at the top, so Howard Hughes was not a temptation. After a moment's pause, trying to think of how to get out of this, Mother said, "No, I think not. You're too rich for me."

Years later, when I was seven, this woman who had turned down Howard Hughes stood at one end of our upstairs hallway while I stood at the other, helping me unwind roll after roll of toilet paper. My Brownie troop leader had told us all to collect empty rolls over the past three months, but I had forgotten. Mother didn't criticize me for forgetting, she just unrolled. My troop was making Christmas tree ornaments for the old folks' home with toilet paper spools and glitter. Between my sudden panic at forgetting the assignment, and my unwillingness to enter fully into the spirit of the whole "Toilet paper roll ornaments always cheer up the elderly," I resigned from the Brownies that summer. I'd only joined to march in the Fourth of July parade anyway.

One afternoon when I was ten, and the early dusk of autumn was closing in, I was playing alone on the sidewalk in front of my house. I pretended that the V created by my first two fingers was a slingshot, and I tossed pebbles through it at passing cars. How this puny action could have broken the windshield of a passing car, I will never understand. But I heard a PING, and then a car pulled over and a large man plunged out of it toward me. I turned on my heels and ran home.

When the irate driver reached our front door, Mother answered the doorbell and faced down the stranger who had chased me back to my house. He demanded my blood. She called up the stairs to me, and I reluctantly came down from my hiding place in my father's bathroom, the only room in the house with a door that locked. I listened, open-mouthed, as she skewered the stranger.

"She's been home all day!" Mother lied, her back stiff with indignation. "This neighborhood is simply swarming with small brown-haired girls."

"But she ran right in here," the man insisted.

"The neighborhood girls have been in and out of this house all day," Mother intoned, steely with strength, and picking a piece of imaginary lint from her navy blue sleeve.

When the man left in frustration, Mother turned to me and said mildly, "So how did you do that?"

My mother didn't criticize my absent-mindedness or my juvenile crime, but she found great fault with my lack of "intellectual curiosity" when I didn't want to learn history and of "intestinal fortitude" when I didn't want to shop for dresses any longer.

When I was fourteen, Mother's lessons became more abstract and conceptual. She told me that if I ever got pregnant to be sure to bring the baby home and she would help me raise it.

"Thanks, Mother, that's very supportive," I said, "but I have a flat chest, greasy hair, braces on my crooked teeth, and you've sent me to an all girls' boarding school, so I think we're pretty safe on that score. Still, I appreciate the sentiment."

One afternoon when Mother was sitting on the chaise longue in her bedroom, darning one of my father's socks, and I was sitting on the floor watching her do it, she told me that if I reached the age of thirty-five without marrying, she expected me to go out and have sex with someone, as it was one of life's experiences that I shouldn't miss.

My mother's fierce loyalty to those she loved, her often irrational opinions, her strange mixture of confidence and insecurity, made her a strong, complex woman. She was another of life's experiences I'm glad I didn't miss.

My parents Richard Lea Kennedy, Jr., and Charlotte Jocelyn Pierson Kennedy at their wedding, June 1940

Part II

Childhood

Scars: My Own and Other People's

Scars were my childhood badges of honor, emblems of courage and adventure. Even if I had cried like a baby when the wound occurred, the scar automatically meant I had been brave. Scars on my knees and elbows meant that I ran everywhere instead of walked, scars on my knuckles meant I rode my bike while showing off, scars on my arms meant I tried to make friends with every animal I met, even the ones who didn't want any more friends, and scars on my face meant a need for the dermatologist as a result of too much sun and salt water at an early age.

I haven't gotten a new scar in a long time. Perhaps I am living too carefully.

My early emotional scars were equally manageable. I was blessed with parents who loved and protected me, structuring my adventures with parental common sense and supervision.

My father taught me a code to use on the phone if I ever needed him. If I was at a friend's house and wanted to come home, I was to tell the friend that I was supposed to check in with my parents at a certain hour. Then I would call and tell Dad I was checking in, which was his cue to ask me certain yes-or-no questions.

He would start with "Are you all right?"

"Noooo!" I'd say (with a disappointed air).

"Do you want to come home now?"

"Yes" (with a touch of defiance).

"Do you want me to come pick you up?"

"Yes" (with bitter resignation).

My yeses and noes were done with dramatic flair so the listening friends wouldn't know I was planning my escape. I'd bang the phone down and grump that my dad was impossible, that he wanted me home now, that I was the most misunderstood and mistreated child on the planet. And then I'd go wait outside for his car to turn into the drive and get me out of there.

Of course, as I grew older my parents couldn't protect me from everything. My internal scars have been caused by losing people I loved and will always miss, and by saying and doing things that I regret and that I would give a lot to undo. But, overall, I'd be a fool to complain. I believe that I have a guardian angel who flaps along behind me just as fast as he can to keep me out of trouble.

When I first studied to become a counselor, I was told that if I wanted to be of any help to my clients I had to keep a certain emotional distance from them. It was all right to feel the client's pain, but I had to learn to stop crying a minute or two before the client stopped crying. I shouldn't blur us together and begin to believe that his reality and his scars were my own.

I worked as a counselor for delinquent youth and their families for thirty years. I saw plenty of other people's scars. People told me about how they hurt each other with malicious skill. The parents who betrayed their children, the children who let their parents down.

I have dealt with clients' scars as honestly and openly as I knew how. I "sat as close to the fire for as long as I could without being burned myself."

The contrast between my parents and the parents of many of my clients is like the warmth of the sun versus the chill of the blizzard. I have been blessed, and I know it.

Jane and Me: A Study in Sibling Rivalry

Jane must have liked me once.

In the flickering frames of an old home movie, taken when she was five and I was two, you can see me teeter on the edge of the sofa, about to fall off onto my head. Jane grabs me by the straps of my overalls and hauls me back.

Me and Jane, Lake Forest, Illinois, 1954

I could always count on Jane to haul me back from certain disaster. But between crises, she regarded me with disdain.

I have no idea what stories Mother told Jane, but I was raised with Mother's complex mythology about the nature of her two daughters. Mother assigned roles to each of us without asking which one we'd like to play, then behaved as though they were real.

"Jane," she told me, "was not a cuddly baby. If I tried to hold her she would struggle to get down. The only way I could snuggle her was if I took her on a ride in a taxicab. Then she'd sit on my lap so she could see out the window.

"You, on the other hand, were different right from the first. Your grandmother could tell. She noticed it when you were just a tiny thing, 'Jocelyn,' she said, 'that child is going to be your comfort and your joy.'"

Mother often said that I was her comfort and her joy. I couldn't see it. I just felt like a kid, trying to grow up.

When I was seven, Mother told me that I could read better than Jane did when she was seven. Being young and stupid, I passed this information on to Jane with a smirk. Jane received it in silence.

Did my mother create the rivalry or did I? Jane was prettier than I was. She had style and excellent taste in clothes. Mother told me that it was too bad I was so long-waisted and had no taste whatsoever. She mentioned that since I had thick calves it was a good thing I had small ankles. One evening, when I was ten, and getting ready to go to Mrs. Woolson's Dancing Class, Mother sat on my bed, watching me get dressed. She looked me up and down and finally managed to say that I had excellent shoulders and that someday I'd be glad I had a short upper lip.

Later, alone in my bedroom, I studied myself in the long mirror on the back of my door and saw nothing but carefully curled hair and a blue dress. There's no denying that the implied comparison to Jane stung.

Jane had a great many friends—both girls and boys. On the other end of the social scale, I had no friends. I played with boys until they grew too old to play with me, but girls made me nervous. I wished I had friends.

In Mother's mythology, it was explained to me, "Jane is the pretty one, but you have personality." I was eleven by that point and wise enough not to smirk, but I passed the information on to Jane nonetheless. I didn't mean any harm by it. As I sat on her bed watching her paint her toenails, I said, "I may have personality, but you sure are pretty."

Jane wasn't silent this time. She turned and screamed at me, "You disgusting, nasty baby! You really think that because Mother likes you best that you actually are better than I am? You're not! You're a toad!"

But Jane was wrong, of course. I wasn't Mother's favorite. She was.

Perhaps the four-year age gap between Jane and me was too broad to span. I wanted Jane to like me, and Jane saw me as poison. The closest we came to talking to each other was:

> Me (hanging around Jane with nothing to do)—"Can I play with you and your friends?"
>
> Jane—"If you go to the kitchen and get me a bunch of grapes on a small plate and a Coke with three ice cubes I'll think about it. Don't forget to wash the grapes."
>
> Me (10 minutes later)—"Here Jane, here are your grapes and Coke. Now can I play?"
>
> Jane—"Not this time. I had to ask you for the grapes and Coke. Maybe next time if I don't have to ask."

However, we weren't always at odds. I remember one interminable Sunday lunch in the semi-dark restaurant of the Deerpath Inn. Jane and I were the only children with a party of six adults. We wore our best clothes and sat in polite silence at the foot of the table as the adults talked to each other.

I don't remember whether the Jello came as part of the salad or as dessert. I do remember that we each had a plate of it arranged into a mountain of quivering, bright green cubes. Without words, Jane caught my eye and indicated that I should look at what her hands were doing in her lap. She had a cube of Jello on her spoon, which she was bending backwards, aimed at the ceiling. The tiny alien vehicle made no noise as it soared upward. I made a small gasp, which I changed to a cough as Mother looked down the table at me.

The cube of Jello didn't quite make it to the ceiling, but fell back to earth somewhere on the dark, patterned carpet.

We tried again. I followed Jane's example step by step, and we both adjusted our charge and trajectory. We fired. Jane's missile stuck to the ceiling above us, and mine arced across the dining room to fall harmlessly in a potted plant.

The waiter, who had been leaning against the wall, made eye contact with us and pushed himself forward to glide in our direction.

Hastily, we replaced our spoons by our plates, sat up straight, and smiled at him.

He stopped at a service tray for a pitcher of water, then refilled all our glasses.

The mythology of our differences simultaneously drove us apart and bonded us. We didn't get along, but we were in this family together.

One evening when our parents were out to dinner, leaving us with our housekeeper Mary, Jane and I began to argue and then to fight. Jane had me down on the floor, sitting on my chest, using two handfuls of my hair as handles to bang my head against the floor. When Mary heard the reverberating thuds of my head, she shouted up the stairs, "What are you two girls doing?"

We replied in unison, "Nothing, Mary." Then we waited in a freeze-action frame for the sound of her footfalls going back to the kitchen.

Toward the end of our childhood, when different boarding schools caused us to spend more time apart than together, our relationship improved.

One summer evening, we went to a teenage pool party, arriving together but soon separated by social sets at either end of the pool. The boys were my pals again, but they thought it would be fun to take my arms and legs and swing me out over the pool. I had on a dress, a watch, my period, and a Kotex. I called out to Jane.

"Jane, help me!"

Like a superhero, Jane was there. "Put her down," she said to the boys, with the same simple menace she used on me.

They put me down. Jane looked at me, slumped on the pool deck, smoothing my skirt down over my legs.

"Are you all right?" she asked.

"Yes, thanks. I'm fine," I replied, grateful to have an older sister.

Having hauled me back to safety once again, by the straps of my figurative overalls, Jane said, "Good," and walked away.

What Not to Do on a Rainy Afternoon

It was the second day of rain, and I was completely out of ideas. Being seven, I could fit across the arms of the chair. I lay there, letting my head and legs droop toward the floor, in hopes that someone in the family would notice and wonder if I had died.

I'd already picked at all the loose threads on the upholstery. I'd stared out the window at the rain. I'd tried to undo my work of last year by now teaching the dog to shake with his right paw instead of his left. We were both exhausted and no nearer to our goal.

Lying there, I listened to my mother's end of a telephone conversation with her friend Mrs. Beidler. It was as boring as the rain. "Umm," she said, and "Yes," she continued, and "Good," she intoned.

Finally, Mother turned to me, covered the phone with her hand, and mouthed the words, "Do you want to go to Frank's house to play? He's inviting you over."

"Do I!!!" Life returned to my limbs. I had a reason to live again.

While Mother fetched our coats and the car keys, I ran around and around in small circles, shouting, "Yippee! Yippee!"

At Frank's house, the world was full of possibilities. We decided on an indoor beanbag war, since there was no longer any snow outside for snowball fights. We claimed our forts—an upended card table for him, and the recessed entry near the front door for me.

My fort was open and lower than Frank's, so I was a pretty easy target. But since neither of us could aim, it didn't matter. We had our piles of beanbags. We winged them back and forth at each other with lethal intent and lousy aim.

Realizing that I wasn't actually hitting Frank, I ran up the three stairs with my armload of beanbags to pepper him from short range. I got in a couple of direct hits over his card table, took several hits myself, and ran out of ammunition. I reversed course and plunged back across the front hall, diving down the three steps to my fort by the door.

A sudden stab of pain in my ankle ended my interest in warfare.

Frank lobbed a few desultory beanbags into my fort, but when there was no response, he came over to see what was the matter.

The ankle didn't hurt much, but I felt sick to my stomach, and Frank couldn't get me to stop crying.

"You can have my fort," he tried, his brow furrowed in alarm, "and all my bean bags."

He placed a beanbag in my hand and invited me to whang him with it.

Nothing worked. I cried uninterruptedly.

Frank, also aged seven, played his ace in the hole. "I think I'd better call your mother," he said.

By the time my mother arrived, I'd finally stopped crying.

"You should take her to the doctor's for an X-ray," Mrs. Beidler advised my mother.

I perked up. That would be dramatic. Maybe Mother would have to carry me into the doctor's office. Maybe I'd get a lollipop for being brave. I'd have an exciting story to tell my friends at school on Monday.

"Yes," I agreed, sniffing slightly. "I think we should."

"Hmm," said Mother, looking at me carefully. "Let's just see if it doesn't get better on its own."

She took me home and put me to bed with a glass of ginger ale and a cake of Ivory soap to carve, telling me to rest my ankle.

I placed the back of my hand dramatically over my eyes.

"If it still hurts when you walk on it in the morning, we'll go to the doctor," Mother said, and left the room.

Disappointingly, when I walked on it in the morning, it hardly hurt at all. However, I was not to be cheated out of being the hero of my own drama.

"It still hurts, Mom," I murmured bravely, when she asked about the ankle's progress.

She sighed and fetched the coats and car keys. With her lips slightly pursed, she drove us to the doctor's, while I looked brightly out the car window humming bits of "Onward Christian Soldiers" under my breath. It was still raining.

"It's broken," Dr. Burgert announced blandly, almost as though he didn't grasp the excitement of it all. He ran his eye over the X-ray. "She'll need to stay overnight at the hospital to get it casted, and to wait while the plaster hardens."

Wow!

Mother apologized to me about not taking my feelings more seriously, and not taking me to the doctor's the day before.

I forgave her with a small sad smile, and surreptitiously scanned the X-ray myself, wondering how it could possibly be broken. My foot wasn't dangling uselessly from the end of my leg.

The hospital stay was all I had hoped for, and more. It smelled of exotic antiseptics, and had long linoleum corridors with mysterious doors leading who knew where. There were a few other children on the ward. Most of them were recovering from surgery, but I was allowed to visit the hardier ones. I got a cast from my toes to my crotch. Mom and Dad brought lollipops. Jane looked impressed.

The glory ended far too soon. The nurses grew tired of my wheelchair races with the other children and discharged me to my parents.

But the warm glow of vindication has lasted all my life.

Rescued

I asked to be excused from a long Sunday lunch of overcooked lamb, mint jelly, and green beans. Permission granted, I took myself outdoors for a walk. Sundays in Illinois in the 1950s were dangerous for eight-year-old children. You could easily die of boredom.

Released from lunch, I walked along the suburban sidewalk until I reached an empty lot with a stand of tall pine trees. I sized them up and began to climb to the top of the tallest one. Branches were so evenly spaced on either side that they formed a ladder even a child could maneuver. I scrambled up, with the joy of competence and strength, and admired the view from the top.

I could see for blocks. I became simultaneously a watcher and a hider: an angel and an Indian Scout.

A breeze brushed my cheek. As the thin top of the tree began to sway, I tightened my hold on its branches. The world began to sway, and my tree felt suddenly fragile, my hold precarious. I couldn't loosen my grip enough to begin my descent. Hands slippery with holding on, my breathing began to come faster. My stomach churned. I waited. I believed in my own immortality and in miracles.

Then, far below me, I saw my father walking along in his three-piece suit, his long overcoat and fedora. How had he known I needed him? How had he known which way I'd gone?

I couldn't call loudly, for fear a deep breath would dislodge me, but I breathed, "Daddy," and he heard.

"Where are you?" he called.

"Up here, at the top of the tree," I whispered, and guided him with small noises until he located me at the top of the highest tree, backlit against the sun.

My father scaled the tree, hand over hand, up the ladder of the branches in his slippery leather shoes, until he reached me. He put his hands outside of my hands on the same branches, and his feet outside of my feet, his body cupping mine. And he walked me down the tree.

In my memory, my father is always dressed in a three-piece suit, with a gold watch in his right vest pocket and a watch chain across his stomach ending with his keys in the left vest pocket. He must have had other clothes. He did, after all, sleep in pajamas and paint the picket fence each summer in khakis and an old shirt, but those were exceptions that seemed to prove the rule of the three-piece suit.

He was an excellent father: loving, reliable, and kind. He taught me my prayers and listened to me say them every night as he put me to bed. He taught me how to shine shoes properly and paid me a dime for every pair of his that I polished.

Every winter he took me to the nearest manmade hill in that flat Midwestern prairie so that I could practice skiing. It was bitterly cold, and the wind blew, unhindered, for a thousand miles.

My father would stand at the bottom of the hill in his three-piece suit, with the long overcoat, and the fedora. Occasionally he would stomp his leather-clad shoes, encased in rubber galoshes, to keep his circulation going. He would wait for me to come down that small hill, shouting hello to him and waving my ski poles over my head. He would wave back at me as I plummeted down the slope over and over. I thought nothing of making him wait.

My father was an observer: careful, predictable, older than most of the fathers of my friends. He watched me skate, and sail, and play baseball, but he didn't do any of these things with me. Except for that one Sunday afternoon when he climbed a tree.

The Invisible

Our house was a grand old Victorian in Lake Forest, a suburb of Chicago—a big house full of nooks and crannies perfect for hiding out with a good book on a rainy day, the large front porch spanned its width, and a barn in the back served as a garage. The barn's hayloft no longer held hay, but contained, instead, an old, dusty sleigh with bells along the length of its traces.

As a child, I spent hours in that sleigh. Urgently, I slapped the reins on the back of my imaginary horse, throwing constant glances behind me at the pack of red-eyed wolves, on a wild ride over the moonlit snow.

Mice had gotten into the sleigh before me, and played their own games in the cracked leather of the upholstered seats. When, in excitement, I bounced on my seat, the whole place stank with the sharp, metallic tang of mouse poop.

After a while, I climbed down from the sleigh and walked across the dusty planks of the floor to the hayloft door. I swung it open, and scared myself by looking down at the driveway below. When that thrill paled, I climbed down the ladder to the half-acre of suburban lawn and trees that lay below.

With my father's help, I had built a tree house in the little wooded area between the barn and the lilac bush at the kitchen door. The branches of my pine tree were too thin to hold much, so the tree house was only a small platform, just large enough to hold either my feet or my bottom. I had nailed short planks to the trunk for a ladder.

With an artful swivel, I could get myself over the rim and onto that platform. I was standing in the crow's nest of a square-rigged ship, the first sailor to spot the broad back of the blowing whale as it surfaced from the deep.

"Thar she blows!" I called to my crewmates on the rolling deck below. I held the tree trunk with one arm and pointed to her spray with the other.

The great ship turned slowly, with a flapping of its huge white sails, in the direction of my pointing arm, and we sailed after the leviathan. I was the first to feel the mist of her spray on my face and to be enveloped in her warm, fishy breath.

My childhood stretched ahead of me as endlessly as the ocean. The shelter of my loving parents created an excruciating boredom. Perhaps boredom is an adult's greatest gift to a child. In desperation, I explored the worlds that only I could see.

"Go outside and play," said my mother, busy writing her history of the Ogden family during the American Revolution.

"Play what?" I whined, draping myself upside down on the sofa.

"Anything..., just take a jacket," she replied, without looking up from her typewriter. She hoped that the jacket would allow me to stay out even if it rained.

She began again to type.

I opened my mouth to object and then closed it.

Today, I thought, I'll go out the front door and see what there is to see. Forsythia bushes lined the boundary between my front yard and the neighbor's property. I crawled into the bushes to make a fairy house in the deep shade.

Twigs became walls. Leaves became the roof. Bark was the table. Pebbles were the fairies' stools. Table set with acorn caps for bowls, I was ready for them all to come home from work and sit down to their supper. I hoped they were bringing the food. I couldn't do everything.

I lay on my stomach, cheek pressed against the mud, and saw the fairy family arrive home. The father, in his bright green cap, carried a pail in each hand, full of seeds and berries. The mother, in her petal apron, carried the sleeping baby, ready to put him in the curved leaf cradle I had made. The other children still had enough energy to laugh, and shout, and push each other over the threshold. They fluttered their wings to keep their balance. They commented to each other about the high ceilings, and the spacious rooms. They nodded to me in approval.

My actual human neighbors were an elderly couple I never saw. Their children, if ever there had been any, were long gone. A copse of scattered trees stood between my house and theirs, and in those trees, on their property, lived the iron statue of a life-sized stag. He must have had antlers once, but now there were just stubs on his forehead. Losing them must have been painful, but it had happened long ago, and I felt sure he had gotten over it by now. From my point of view, it was a blessing. What cowboy ever wrangled steers and fought off Indians while squinting through a pair of antlers?

I practiced running at that deer, grabbing one of his iron ears, and swinging myself onto his back, until I could do it in seconds. I lived much of my childhood on his back: butt chillingly cold in winter, and hot to the touch in summer.

The forsythia bushes, with their long straight runners, could supply a thick branch for a bow, and slender branches for the arrows. The leaves overhead cast moving shadows all around me. Those movements became handsome sheriffs and greedy stagecoach robbers, tame eagles and hungry bears.

I went back into the house, where the light was dimly filtered through sheer curtains, and the air was far too still. My friends didn't step through the door with me. The upholstered furniture and highly polished dining table would have suffocated them. They waited for me in the trees.

"Mom, where's the string?" I shouted.

"Why do you want it?" came her reply from upstairs.

"To string my bow."

"In the center drawer of the kitchen table," she called back.

With string and the good kitchen knife, I escaped outdoors again. Bow strung, I leaned sideways down my horse, legs wrapped tightly around his sides, and shot my arrows from beneath his neck. I brought down one buffalo from the thundering herd of a thousand. Their broad brown backs stretched uninterruptedly as far as my eyes could see.

Later, when I grew hungry, I carried one heavy stone at a time until I'd built a ring, and filled it with dry sticks and leaves for tinder.

Another trip into the house.

"Mom," I yelled up the stairs, "I need matches and some food to cook on my campfire."

"The matches are on the stove, and you can wrap bacon around a stick. Don't burn the woods down."

"I won't," I shouted. I took my supplies and returned outdoors.

From among my friends, I motioned to my guardian angel, a giant of a man with unruly red-brown hair and wings folded smoothly along his back. He rose from the stump where he was playing Rock, Paper, Scissors with the children of the fairy family.

"Stay close to me please, just in case," I requested.

He nodded his assent. As I lit the match, he cupped his hands around mine, holding them until the pile of dry leaves caught, then leaned in to blow out the match before the flame reached my fingers.

My mother's benign neglect was my salvation. With my imaginary friends, reality lost the power to be the sole judge of who I was. They knew me as a dependable sailor, a competent house builder, an honest cowboy, a brave Indian, and an animal whisperer.

I wanted to be the person my imaginary friends believed I was.

They became the moral compass that I carried. They gave me the courage to survive school days filled with tribulations: the wrong clothes that attracted the disdain of other little girls, the wrong answer that created an explosion of laughter from the entire class, the wrong teacher who saw no potential.

My friends couldn't enter the school building, but they waited for me just outside.

Our old Victorian, Lake Forest, Illinois

The Rowboat—Part One, 1957

Dear Ben,

This is a combination of love letter and thank you letter to tell you how important a part of my life you are, and why. I figure that since you've been dead almost thirty-six years, you have by now developed enough heavenly equilibrium to be able to take compliments without discomfort. If not, then what have you been doing with your time?

By getting to know you when I was eleven and you were forty-two, I discovered that paying attention to someone else not only satisfied my curiosity but calmed and completed me. That first summer, when I ran barefoot down to the harbor to see John Linehan, the Sailing Master, I found you there as well, his old childhood friend and newly hired assistant. I will admit that the first thing I noticed was that you were quite possibly the handsomest man I'd ever seen: reddish blond hair cut short, tanned arms and legs, and deep blue eyes. The second thing I noticed was that you seemed shy, thoughtful of speech, and gentle of manner. And the third thing was that you were different from other adults. There was some mystery about you, and I wanted more than anything to figure it out. I was hungry for understanding adults the way a rooster is hungry for the sunrise, or a drip on the window is hungry for the sill.

I was accustomed to the general run-of-the-mill, stalwart, decent adult who fobs children off with platitudes or half-truths, who doesn't have time or inclination to tell them what the children don't even know they want to know. John Linehan was one of these, with a wife and family and responsibility for dozens of children who wanted to learn to sail but couldn't even swim yet, much less follow instructions well enough to survive a summer on the ocean in a small boat. He was "black Irish," with a charm that made him easy to love, and Irish moods that could switch from calm to storm in the blink of an eye. He was the sun and the moon to me, but he was predictable, and he belonged to too many other people.

But you, Ben, you didn't belong to anyone yet, and I wanted you to belong to me.

I had rules for myself in the occupation of getting to know adults, which had been figured out by making all the possible mistakes.

> Rule I—Never ask an adult who isn't your parent for anything for yourself. If you do, the adults will invariably look at their watches and exclaim, "Just look at the time. Aren't you supposed to go home?"

> Rule II—Never ask any adult a difficult personal question or they will say, "You'll understand that when you're older."

> Rule III—Never expect anything from an adult, and you won't be disappointed.

I assume that you knew I was stalking you that summer. It would have been difficult to miss. I wonder what you made of it all. Thank you for being such an honorable man. I would guess that being stalked by a scrawny, lonely, nearly-mute child was a challenge, but you pulled it off. You never made me feel stupid or silly. You never sent me home, you never told me to go outside and play, and, possibly because I never asked you a question, you told me a heartful.

In your off-hours from teaching sailing, you worked on an old rowboat. You had pulled it up on the beach about twenty-five yards from the pier and were intent on restoring it. I was intent on hanging out with you, and the rowboat made that possible.

At first we said very little. I would just join you as you worked. Occasionally, while reaching for the paint scraper, you'd muse something like, "I wonder if this old boat will ever float again. She's dry as dust," not looking directly at me, not expecting a response.

I'd nod and look thoughtful, as though I were weighing the boat's chances of revival. If effort makes boats float, this one would be a success. And anyway, you thought it would work, Ben, so I did too.

An hour might pass and you'd say, "Where's the screwdriver?" and I'd feel around in the sand with my toes to locate where it had rolled off the hull onto the beach unnoticed. We were a good team, working together in companionable silence. Well, you were working and I was looking at my toes, or the boat, or the sky.

As the days passed, you taught me how to help scrape off the old paint and how to pull caulking delicately from between the planks. Along with the progress on the boat, our relationship grew easier. It became accepted that you and I would work on the rowboat after the tasks of the day were done. You didn't have to focus all your attention on the rowboat, and I didn't have to pretend that I was about to think of something to say.

We must have chatted together a bit, but that's not what I remember. I remember an easy silence with very few words getting in our way. One day you mentioned that you had three sons, two older than I was, and one two years younger. The oldest one was in college, and the two younger ones were attending boarding schools.

> Rule IV—Never express surprise at what an adult
> tells you or they'll notice you're there.

I followed my rule, but I was taken aback when you told me about your youngest son. If I hadn't already been silent, it would have robbed me of speech. I knew I wouldn't be going away to boarding school until I was fourteen, and your nine-year-old was already there. Why? I didn't ask you, because it wouldn't have been right, but I chewed on this puzzle for some time.

Another day, as you sanded the planks smooth, you told me that you were divorced, and I mentally added this piece to the puzzle. I don't remember the context of this conversation, although it must have had one. But that was the information I got, no more, no less. And I wondered, if your youngest son's mother didn't want him with her, why wasn't he with you?

Weeks passed. The littlest kids began to graduate from rowing to sailing in their morning classes, and then move on to the intricacies of landing at the dock or at a mooring. The sky was always blue, the water always warm and green, and the sails were always full of wind. In the afternoons, I raced as crew with older kids who had their own boats. Then, after the sailboats were home and moored, I'd work on the rowboat with you.

We'd worked most of the caulk out from between the boards, with a minimum of splintering of the wood. And now began the slow delicate task of inserting new cotton caulking, easing it between the boards with screwdrivers. One day, while asking me to hand you the hammer, you mentioned that you lived with your mother. Again I was surprised but silent. It had never occurred to me to wonder why you had the entire summer free, and had the time to become John's Assistant Sailing Master, but it filled another hole in the jigsaw puzzle, a missing piece I hadn't known to look for.

One particularly hectic morning, I was helping you and John Linehan fend off the little kids as they tried to bring their boats in for a landing at the dock. They came at speeds guaranteed to sheer their forestays and possibly their masts if they weren't stopped. They came from all angles, ignoring the wind direction, just praying to land safely. We rushed from one side of the pier to the other, catching hold of the masts and using the boats' own momentum to swing them back out to try again—only from downwind this time.

You and I stopped for a moment to catch our breath. It would take time for the kids to land again. Leaning on one of the pilings, you looked far across the water and said, "About the worst feeling in the world is to be able to see and hear everything, but to be frozen into a body that won't respond in any way. And then to have the men come and take you away, and you can see everyone's faces as you go."

I'm glad we were outside in the sunshine. We needed space and light for that memory. And now the puzzle was becoming whole. The shyness, the nine-year-old in boarding school, the divorce, the living with your mother, the memory of being taken away by men. I got it. You had been crazy and you were better now, but still different.

From my point of view, your difference made you better, but you might not have thought so.

At the end of the summer, I asked if I could write you, and you said yes.

We had a correspondence of twenty years, one more summer sailing, and brief visits together before you died. There's a quote by John Donne that applies to us: "More than kisses, letters mingle souls."

You let me get to know you, slowly, gradually, never overwhelming me with too much or pushing me away with too little. As I got to know you better, I realized that what I love about you is that you incorporate that rare combination of brave and kind. And as I got to know you, I also got to know me. I learned that of all the human virtues, those two are the most important. Intelligence, humor, talent are frosting on the cake. What I want to be is brave and kind.

I also learned from you that patience and unlimited perseverance, like those of a young child, may eventually be rewarded with learning about another person. I discovered that what I really wanted was to spend my life following that thread of interest and attention wherever it led, with anyone willing to let me in.

At the end of the summer, you patted the hull of the rowboat and said, "She's as ready as she'll ever be. Let's try her in the water."

You and I righted her and dragged her in about knee deep, and watched with concern as she filled up with seawater faster than a bath with the tap on.

"Hmmm," you said slowly. "Perhaps the caulk needs time to swell. We'll leave her underwater overnight and try again tomorrow."

I smiled at you with satisfaction that our dilemma had a reason and probably a solution. We went to our homes, and to our suppers, feeling at peace with the world.

Early the next morning, we met at the water, lugged the boat high enough to tip the water out of her, and then floated her again. This time, she sank even faster. The water poured in from a dozen leaks, and the wood was not even faintly buoyant.

We just looked at each other, and slowly began to laugh.

"Well," you said, grinning, "It's a good thing the pleasure was in the doing, and not in the final result."

I smiled at you, and nodded my agreement.

Love,
Laura

Ben Hallowell, by Laura de Blank, watercolor on paper, 2015

Credo

Waking in the dark before dawn, I believe in God
Jumping out of bed at first light, I am baptized a Presbyterian
Running downstairs to breakfast, I know there is life after death
Chewing scrambled eggs and toast, I learn the Lord's Prayer to
    collect the 25 cents my father promised me

Walking slowly to school through the dried autumn leaves, I accept
    the idea of heaven, and dismiss hell
Sitting at my school desk parsing sentences and splitting infinitives, I
    recognize that, except for believing in the afterlife, I am Jewish
Chasing the ball at recess, my shirttails flapping, I try to contact the
    dead, with limited success
Eating the school's boiled lunch, I give up organized religion

Chewing on my pencil in Study Hall, reading about trains
    simultaneously leaving Chicago and New York, I understand that
    animals go to Heaven too
Walking home through the darkening afternoon, my shoelaces
    untied, I realize that faith means "without proof"
Eating steak and potatoes with my family in the yellow-lit dining
    room, I decide that if there is no proof, I might as well believe in
    the reassuring over the alarming

Getting into my sagging bed between the clean crisp sheets, I choose
    to believe that God loves us all and that He has a plan

Old Friendships

"I really didn't want to see you again," Charlotte said to me in a gentle voice.

The Phoenix restaurant was almost filled, but the hostess showed us, two women in their sixties, to a table in the back.

"It took me a long time to decide to meet you for lunch," she murmured, so softly it was hard to hear.

"Yes, I figured as much," I replied, sitting down and pulling in my chair, "when you didn't come to our grade school reunion in Lake Forest."

"You were my only friend," Charlotte said, looking at her hands. "Why would I want to see the others?"

"Well, you were my only friend too," I replied, looking at the anxious expression on her face.

Long ago, Charlotte and I had been bonded together as children by the realization that we were visible to each other, while recognizing, without words, that we were invisible to our classmates.

I had only travelled back to Illinois for the 50th reunion because my husband Paul shamed me into it. He told me it was time to face the monsters of my childhood, and to see them all with adult eyes. That didn't work particularly well, but while I was there, I learned that Charlotte had moved to Phoenix two years before. It took many phone calls to persuade her to meet me for lunch.

I still recognized Charlotte, although I hadn't seen her in fifty years. As a child, she was tall and stocky, with a permanent scowl on her face. She was still tall, with a comfortable old lady spread to her waist. Her scowl had eased, leaving a look of puzzlement around her eyes.

*   *   *   *

My family lived close to town, while Charlotte's lived far out in the country, surrounded by cornfields. It was difficult for us to get together to play. A mother had to drive one of us. I realize now, looking back, that I always went to Charlotte's house, often staying the night, and my mother would come back to fetch me the next day. Charlotte and I played with her dogs, explored the woods, and ran through the tall rows of corn, pretending we were in a maze. We did homework, watched TV, and slipped quietly into her father's library to study his *Playboy* magazines.

Her parents were usually at home, although I seldom saw them. Occasionally, one or the other would stick a head in the door to see if we were still there. We certainly never ate with them; they always seemed to be dressed in glittering clothes and on their way to a party. The cook fed us in the kitchen.

Charlotte's mother and father had each been married and divorced before, and each had a son by those previous marriages. Then they'd married each other and had two more children: Charlotte and Chammie, her little brother. The big brothers were much older, and away at school when we were young.

I knew all this because everyone knew it, but what I didn't know, and possibly Charlotte didn't understand, either, at that age, was that her father was an alcoholic, and her mother, perhaps out of a sense of competition, didn't like girls or women. I never saw anyone hit Charlotte, but every time I went to her house, I could sense the anger that pervaded it. Charlotte's mother never missed a chance to tell her she was a disappointment and an embarrassment, and then she'd look at me, as if we shared this opinion.

I just went blank. Being ten, I knew her saying that was wrong, but it was so far outside my own experience that I didn't know what to do.

It was impossible for Charlotte to recognize abuse for what it was, as she was the only girl in the family, and singled out for it.

Charlotte's early scowl grew into a simmering rage. One morning in fourth grade, Miss Compton, walking along the aisles of desks, told us to get out our history books and turn to page 148.

Perhaps I missed something, but I wasn't prepared when she reached Charlotte, and my friend slammed her book down upon her desk, shouting, "NO!" in Miss Compton's face.

The air became thick and painful. Charlotte continued to yell almost wordlessly. This scene was far beyond anything I had known. From my desk across the room, pressed small in my chair, I watched my friend.

Miss Compton told Charlotte to go to Principal Bell's office. Charlotte screamed, "NO!"

The rest of us watched but didn't move.

Miss Compton told Jimmy to get Mr. Bell. Jimmy ran. The stalemate between Charlotte and Miss Compton continued.

I failed Charlotte that day, just as I had in her home when her mother insulted her. It didn't occur to me to go to her. If I had gone to stand beside her, even if I'd been blown to bits by her rage, would that have helped?

Mr. Bell arrived and, with the arrogance of the customarily obeyed, ordered Charlotte to follow him out of the room. Charlotte screamed her refusal. Mr. Bell pulled at her arm.

There was a momentary lull in the yelling, as Charlotte leaned forward and wrapped her arms around her desk. It was the old-fashioned kind where the seat is permanently attached to the heavy-lidded desk.

Mr. Bell put his arms around Charlotte's waist and pulled. She did not let go. Her fingers turned white.

We watched Mr. Bell drag Charlotte and her desk across the room. She shouted a long, wordless snarl. She let her hair fall forward, so we could no longer see her red, tear-stained face.

When the desk got stuck in the doorway, Mr. Bell gave a tremendous tug, fueled by his own temper. Losing her hold, Charlotte was yanked out of the classroom.

Charlotte didn't return to class that day, and when she and I saw each other again, we didn't talk about what happened. We just returned to our lives. But we had changed. Now Charlotte knew what she was capable of. I discovered there were levels of emotion I hadn't known existed.

*　　　*　　　*　　　*

After the waitress brought our sandwiches, Charlotte said, "Did you know my mother took me to see a psychiatrist once when I was a child?"

"No," I replied. "How did that go?"

"I don't really know. I remember sitting for a long time in his waiting room while he talked to my mother. He gave me a piece of paper and a pen and told me to entertain myself by drawing pictures. I drew the same small horse heads that I used to draw on everything at that age, and when he came back and saw them he asked me why they were so small. I just looked at him in surprise, as it had never occurred to me to draw them any bigger.

"He talked to me and mother together for a while, and then he told me to go to the waiting room again, while he talked to my mother alone.

49

"I didn't see him again. Mom just came out and told me it was time to go. In the car on the ride home, I asked her what he had said was wrong with me."

"What did she say?" I asked.

Charlotte smiled almost imperceptibly and said, "Apparently he said there was nothing wrong with me, and gave her the name of another therapist that she should see herself. Neither of us ever went to a psychiatrist again."

"I'm glad he told her that."

"Did you know how my mother died?" Charlotte continued, turning from me to look out the window. "Some years after I married, my parents went on a cruise to the Orient together, and my mother died on-board of a massive stroke. Somehow they were able to refrigerate her body on the ship and continue the cruise. My father was engaged to marry another woman before they docked in San Francisco."

I just nodded. There was nothing to say to that. We had both known her parents and what they were like.

But I hadn't been their girl child.

The waitress brought us our bill, and Charlotte and I spent a few minutes dividing it up and figuring out the tip.

"When am I going to get over all of this, Laura?" Charlotte asked, rising from her chair and putting her napkin on the table. "It happened decades ago and it still haunts me."

I rose with her. "You never believed your parents, Charlotte. You always fought back. Your rage was right," I said, reaching out to hug her. "You were powerful. I saw your parents being mean to you. I just didn't know what to do about it."

She hugged me back.

"I'm sorry," I said, as we walked together out of the restaurant.

We made a date to eat lunch the following week. Charlotte smiled, and we separated to our cars.

Jellyfish

At the age of fourteen, I saw myself as a spineless jellyfish, not an attractive and dangerous jellyfish like the iridescent Portuguese Man-of-War. That one rides the surface of the water, using his balloon as a sail, to maneuver lethal tentacles close to prey. No, I was the harmless and transparent Four-Leaf-Clover jellyfish that simply drifts in and out with every tide.

I had been in school with the same girls for eleven years, ever since junior kindergarten. All of them disliked me, and therefore I disliked them in return. When there had been boys in our class, we girls had gotten along with less drama. But when the boys left for their respective boarding schools at the end of eighth grade, they left a class of nine girls waiting another year before we would leave as well. My life got much worse in ninth grade.

Just because I told my parents that I didn't like my classmates didn't mean that was strictly true. If they had liked me, I would have liked them very much. It would have been proof of their discerning taste and good sense. As it was, I realized they were shallow and mean. I would have given my eyeteeth to fit in, and thrown in a few molars if I could have been popular. But I was nerdy: different, but without the courage to pull it off. I tried repeatedly to dance to a tune I could not hear, by watching where others put their feet.

I spent half my time sullenly disdaining my classmates, and the other half trying to get them to like me, which confused all of us.

One early spring afternoon, I walked down a long school corridor with two other girls, going from one class to another. As we passed the open door of the teachers' lounge, my classmates talked loudly about how much they hated Mr. Lindahl, the Latin teacher, a pale, plump young man, whose green waterproof book-bag the girls had periodically stuffed with icicles throughout the winter.

Without thinking of the repercussions, I said, "Shhh." I thought he might be in the lounge, would hear them, and get his feelings hurt.

"What did you say?" they asked menacingly.

"Well," I sniped back, "if you had let me finish my word, you'd know I was going to say 'Shit,' before you so rudely interrupted me."

"Oh," they both said noncommittally. They went back to ignoring me, and I returned to self-loathing.

Mr. Ward taught Ancient History. His only real interests, as far as I could tell, were coaching the boys' football teams and reminiscing about his experiences during the Korean War.

Mr. Ward taught history to both the seventh and ninth grades. With the logic of early adolescence, we ninth-graders decided that since we didn't like him, we should cheat on his final exam. I don't know why the seventh grade decided to cheat, too. Perhaps they were the younger brothers and sisters of my classmates, and thought it was a sophisticated crime to commit.

It was a simple form of cheating. All nine girls in my class agreed to bring our study notes into the cafeteria, where the exam was held, and refer to them as needed. This method presupposes that you have studied hard enough to have lots of notes to cheat from, but whether we knew the material was not the point. The point was our adolescent disdain.

So I studied and prepared lots of notes, which I put at the back of the pad of paper we each brought into the exam room. We didn't have exam books then, but used a pad for answering the questions. I flipped back and forth from the front of the pad to the back throughout the exam, looking up the exact names and dates. We seemed to get away with it.

Then, two days later, the seventh grade snitched on us. The news raced through the school. We heard we were in trouble hours before it arrived.

Mr. Mason was our headmaster. He was the man who had taught me sixth-grade arithmetic, who had given me a gift-wrapped box of tiddlywinks that Christmas to remind me to pay more attention to my decimal points, the man who was a personal friend of my father's, and a man I loved. He entered our classroom in the middle of the French lesson and asked our teacher to let him address the class.

Mr. Mason pulled the teacher's chair out from behind the desk and sat down directly in front of us. I was sitting in the back row, but when you are in a class of only nine girls, there's nowhere to hide. He explained that the seventh grade had admitted to cheating and implicated us as well.

"I'm here to ask you about it," he said.

No one spoke.

The silence stretched out and tears began to run down my face. Mr. Mason could see me, but at least my classmates were all facing forward, and I was careful not to sniff. I couldn't wait there until my tears caused him to ask me what they meant. I stood up, and carefully keeping my back to my classmates, I walked past Mr. Mason and out of the room. He let me go without comment. I looked up and down the empty halls, then fled to that old sanctuary, the girls' bathroom, and locked myself in a stall.

Finally, I breathed again. I was safe. I had water and a toilet. I could stay there until nightfall and then slip out the window. In the meantime, Mr. Mason couldn't come in here because he was a man.

Instead, he sent a girl from one of the younger grades in after me. I was standing on the toilet seat, holding my breath, when a girl's voice said, "Laura?"

Naturally, I said, "What?"

"Mr. Mason wants to talk to you."

Numb, I climbed down off the toilet and slid the bolt back on the stall door. Without words, the girl led me down the hall to a small office that Mr. Mason had commandeered for this interview. The girl withdrew. It was just the two of us, him sitting and me standing before him.

"Did you cheat?" he asked calmly.

"Yes."

"Why?"

"Because everyone else did."

"Do you understand that I have to give you an F for the entire year of Ancient History?"

"Yes, I suppose so."

"And it's not just that," he continued. "You must go home now and tell your mother, and I must call Concord Academy and tell them what you've done. You know that you're accepted there for next year on the condition of your successful completion of this year, but I'll try to explain that this F shouldn't cause them to withdraw your acceptance."

I would have loved to have thrown myself on Mr. Mason's broad tweedy chest and mumbled, "Remember the tiddlywinks." But I knew I had grown too old for that. I was in serious trouble, and I was expected to pull my own weight as we sought to get me out of it.

Eddie Dugan, the school janitor, and all-around children's friend, drove me home in uncharacteristic silence. I let myself into the cool, dark house and climbed the stairs to my mother and father's bedroom.

I could hear Mother on the phone to someone as I approached. I stood before her and waited until she hung up before telling her why I was home at 1:30 in the afternoon.

I don't know what Mr. Mason said to Concord Academy, but they let me enter in spite of the F on my transcript. And although I never discussed it with my classmates, they all seemed to go to their designated schools, too.

Somehow Mr. Mason saved us all.

I was still fourteen when I arrived at boarding school in the fall, alone and lost. There were a hundred girls in this school instead of nine, and no boys. But at least these were different girls.

I looked around my dorm room, studying the yellow and gray pattern of amorphous shapes on the New England wallpaper. Sitting down on my bed, I opened the information packet I'd been given: a welcome note, a hand-drawn map of the campus, and my class schedule. There, at the head of the list, was Ancient History. It was even being taught with the same textbook I'd had last year. Clearly, it might make sense to some people that if you flunk a course, you have to take it again, but this was all just so unfair!

I straightened my embryonic spine, walked over to the administration building, and requested an interview with Mrs. Phelps, the intimidating Assistant Head Mistress.

The low September light streamed in the windows while we had a strange conversation in her dark-paneled office. I wonder what Mrs. Phelps made of it. I stood on the Oriental rug in front of her desk and explained my dilemma with Ancient History. I told her that I quite understood her mistake, and that anyone might think that a girl who failed Ancient History in ninth grade should take it again in tenth.

"But you see," I explained patiently, "I didn't fail it because I didn't know it. I failed it because I cheated on the exam."

Mrs. Phelps was a bit like Mr. Mason. Perhaps she liked adolescents.

After a long pause, during which she held my gaze with careful scrutiny, she said, "All right. I'll switch you to American History."

I walked out of her office and back to my room. I had no one to tell about my success, but I sat on the bed and reviewed it. Suddenly, the wallpaper didn't seem so grim. It looked almost like a pattern of jellyfish.

I sat down on the floor between my bed and the wall, and with my new No. 2 pencil carefully began to draw in a spine for each one.

Homesick

I arrived at boarding school at age fourteen, never having been away from home, even for sleep-away camp.

I had been looking forward to going away. For one thing, it was inevitable. Every child I knew went to boarding school. The boys left after eighth grade and the girls after ninth. For another thing, I hadn't been particularly happy in ninth grade, and was looking forward to meeting some new girls. Fourteen was young to be entering sophomore year of high school, but I had wanted to start kindergarten at four, and my family had let me.

My mother flew with me on that first flight from Chicago to Boston, and then we took a cab to Concord, Massachusetts. I began to feel funny on that taxi ride. The scenes out the car window appeared distant and blurred. I was too old to hold my mother's hand, but she stroked my arm during the entire trip. I didn't object. She was my lifeline.

We arrived at Concord Academy, and found the house I would be living in. The burly taxi driver carried my suitcase and school trunk to the front hall. Mother and I took them upstairs to the room I would share with two other girls, and made my bed with the sheets and blankets from the trunk.

Mother helped me unpack my clothes, hanging skirts and dresses in the closet and folding underwear, shirts, and socks in the drawers of the old, scarred dresser. I didn't want to leave my room, which was filled with the presence of my mother taking care of me. But when there was nothing more to do, she led me back downstairs to the hall, filled with milling girls chattering like sparrows, their words indistinguishable.

Upon being introduced to another mother in the crowd of mothers, mine let out a little shriek of pleasure and grasped the woman's hand, saying, "Eleanor, how are you? I haven't seen you since we were in elementary school on Long Island!"

An old-girl carrying a clip board approached me where I was standing close to my mother, and asked if I would like to join her and Eleanor's daughter, Marian, along with some other new girls in observing the first student council meeting of the year. My mother gave me a little push, saying, "Yes, go, go," and turned back to her friend.

I asked the old-girl how long this would take, and she said, "About an hour." Reluctantly, I left my mother's side, assuring her, in case she became worried about me, that I would rejoin her, right there, in an hour.

It was a very boring student council meeting. I think this was a ploy that the school had developed over the decades to separate the new girls from their mothers. Rather like getting the calves away from the cows to make branding possible. My mother was harder-hearted than a cow. She wasn't waiting outside the corral, bellowing for me.

When I was allowed out of the meeting, I rushed back to the hall, only to be told that my mother's friend Eleanor had given her a lift to the airport for her flight back to Chicago. The two mothers had left messages for Marian and me. "Be good. Take care. See you at Thanksgiving."

The rest of the day was total chaos. I followed the other girls to the dining hall, frightened that I would never find my dormitory again. Other girls either knew each other, or were simply quick to make friends. I was drowning in a sea of high-pitched voices. Eventually, the day ended, and by asking around, I found my dorm.

I went upstairs to my room, smiled at my two roommates, who didn't say much either, and got my pajamas out of the drawer where my mother had placed them. Taking my bag of toilet articles down the hall to the bathroom, I brushed my teeth and stared at myself in the mirror. It was good to see a familiar face.

I climbed into bed, lying on the sheets my mother had smoothed out and tucked in. I rolled to the edge and slid my hand between the mattress and the springs. My mother's hand had been there, so in a way I was holding her hand.

During the days that followed, I went to all my classes, usually getting lost on the way. I cried uninterruptedly, and found that carrying a few Kleenex in my pockets was inadequate. Within minutes, they were soaked, reduced to hard, sodden pellets. I had to carry the entire box of tissues with me everywhere.

I'm sure I wasn't the only new girl who was homesick and going through a mild psychotic break, but I was certainly the wettest.

I wrote my parents a letter. "I know you thought that sending me away to school would be in my best interest, but it isn't. Bring me home," I demanded. "I am miserable."

They wrote back. "I'm glad you miss us. We didn't raise you for fourteen years just to have you leave home without a backward glance. We miss you too, but no, you aren't coming home. Hang in there. You'll adjust."

My parents had gone through Jane's homesickness when my sister had gone away to her boarding school three years before. They felt that telephone calls had made it worse, so they told me not to call home until I felt better. In the meantime, we wrote letters.

Finally, on a Saturday afternoon in November, I felt I could talk to my parents without sobbing, so I called them. My father answered, and I said, "Hi, Dad. It's Laura."

There was a gulp at the other end, and he said, "Laura, where are you?"

"I'm still where you put me, Dad. Where did you think I'd be? At the corner drugstore?" I was a bit snarky, but after all, they'd sent me away.

There was a strangled silence on the phone, and I said, "Dad? Dad?"

"Yes, I'm here," he replied between sobs.

I tried to talk to him. I really did. But he couldn't speak for sobbing, making his words unintelligible. I told him about school as cheerfully as I could, but when I ran out of things to say, and he hadn't stopped crying, I asked to speak to my hard-hearted mother.

An Innocent Abroad

During the summer of 1962, when I was sixteen and had finished my junior year at Concord Academy, Jane was invited to go on a two-week cruise of the Greek Islands with her friend June Laflin and June's parents. To my surprise, at the last minute I was included in this plan, and the five of us set off.

The ship had originally run coal from Newcastle to wherever coal was shipped. Having eventually retired from that career, it had been bought by the Greek government, scrubbed very clean, refitted with staterooms, and turned into a tourist liner.

The trip was filled with sunshine, handsome Greek sailors almost universally named Costas, and stops at the ports of blue and white hillside villages. I paid a price for going on this trip, however, Jane's sense of humor being what it was.

One evening after dinner, when all the passengers were sitting on straight-backed chairs around the edges of the dance floor listening to the five-piece band, the musicians stopped playing, and the band leader announced, in several languages, that he had been told there was a famous guitarist among the guests, who was going to play for everyone. He then moved one lone chair out into the middle of the room, signaled for silence, and laid his guitar gently on the empty chair.

The room stilled in anticipation. The bandleader walked across the dance floor and came to stand directly in front of me. He took my limp hand, ignored my dazed look, and led me to the empty chair, seating me and handing me the guitar.

Like a zombie, I sat there holding an instrument I didn't play. I had received four lessons on it as a child, and had almost mastered Elvis's "Love Me Tender," when the guitar teacher stopped showing up.

I glanced at the ring of faces around the room, all happy and attentive, until my eyes found my sister's. She was trying so hard to keep a straight face that her eyes were watering. I placed the guitar gently on the floor beside me, and looking neither left nor right, I fled.

I didn't go all the way back to the tiny bedroom we shared. Instead, I waited in the hallway. It took almost an hour for Jane to emerge, but I knew she would have to come out of that ballroom eventually. Being incapable of thinking of a clever revenge, I settled for beating the crap out of her, only stopping when we were both winded.

Another day, Jane got to breakfast before me. I should have known better than to let her do that. The passengers all sat at long, family-style tables, and when I arrived, Jane was just leaving. I took her empty seat at the table with a nice American woman and her five children. Before I could get the first forkful of scrambled egg to my mouth, the mother started peppering me with Bible questions. How old was Methuselah when he died? How many angels can dance on the head of a pin? What were the names of Jesus's brothers and sisters? The questions came fast, and I was having trouble making up plausible answers. Always eager to please, I began to count the siblings off on my fingers,

"Let's see, there was little Mary and Joe Junior," I mumbled.

The woman rose from her chair with a sniff of disdain and said, "Well, I don't think you know a lot for the Midwestern Bible Scholar Champion of 1961. Your sister said these questions would be easy for you."

Needless to say, I tried to meet new people, and to stay as far away from Jane as a small ship would allow. That's how I met the Cornetets, Marthe and her husband Alain, a French couple from Reims who had left their four children at home with a nanny and come on holiday. They spoke no English.

I knew from my mother's vague threats that she was planning to have me spend a summer with a French family, and she had already asked her cousin Isabelle, who lived in Paris, to find one. I figured that if this plan were inevitable, at least I could find the family myself. I liked Marthe Cornetet. She was patient with my schoolgirl French. She had the uncanny ability to anticipate what I was trying to say and supply the word I was looking for. She had young children. Perhaps she needed a babysitter. I could improve my French with people I liked, doing a job I could learn to do.

Toward the end of the two weeks, when our return to Piraeus was imminent, I knew I had to make my move. I sat myself down on an empty deck chair next to Marthe and asked her if she needed a young girl "pour soigner vos enfants?" Apparently soigner means to "look after" in the sense of to "nurse." Marthe gently untangled my sentence and surmised that I was looking for work as a babysitter. "Garder, pas soigner," she corrected.

Perhaps she was sorry for the public humiliation of a girl who couldn't play the guitar, because she said yes, I could come. She and I arranged that I would ask my mother when we joined her in Paris, and I would come to Marthe in a week or two if it were approved.

Mother was a bit nonplussed. This was moving faster than she had anticipated. She talked it over with Cousin Isabelle, who sent her chauffeur, Vladimir, a terrific snob, to scope out the Cornetet family in their little village of Jonchery Sur Vesle, just outside of Reims. Vladimir duly grilled the Cornetets and returned to Isabelle reporting that Alain Cornetet was the village doctor, with his office on the ground floor of his house, that the family seemed respectable, and most important, of course, that their French was good.

I moved in with the Cornetets in July, planning to stay for two weeks, and instead stayed for six. I returned for the next four summers.

Marthe was the linchpin of the family, warm and generous, a sharp contrast to her husband Alain, who was cold and remote. He was probably a good doctor, but the only warmth he had he kept for very young girls—not his own daughters, but young housemaids were fair game. I kept my eyes on the floor when he was around, and made sure never to be alone with him. When I had a cold one summer, he offered to administer a suppository. I said, "No, thanks. I'll keep the cold." Possibly that is a traditional French remedy for a head cold, but I didn't trust him.

Of the four children, Martine was nine that first summer, Pierre eight, Veronique seven, and Vincent a brown-eyed two. Marthe did all the cooking, and a young woman came every day to clean and help with the children, so they didn't really have work for me. But I helped with whatever I could find that needed doing.

I learned how to éplucher the haricots verts, and to stuff the snail shells with garlic butter before pushing the snail in with my thumb. I sat at the kitchen table while Marthe cooked, learning the mysteries of homemade salad dressing and yoghurt. I changed Vincent's diapers and told the children innumerable stories about Charlie, an American boy who loved baseball.

Martine was a little mother, and took good care of me as well as her siblings.

Pierre was determined to teach me the genders of French nouns, but kept switching the object he was pointing at. He'd point to his leg, and I would say, "*la* jambe." He would smile and say, "No, *le* genou/the knee." On we went with everything we saw.

Seven-year-old Veronique was affectionate and tended to want to sit on my lap or at least hang on me. It was a hot summer and I needed space.

"Ca te gêne?" she asked, hanging her full weight on my shoulder.

"Non," I replied, not sure of the meaning of the verb gêner. It meant either to please or to bother. I had a fifty-fifty chance of telling her that her limp, damp tendency to hang on me was unacceptable.

After my "Non," she smiled and continued to hang.

"Ca te gêne?" means "Does this bother you?" It was permanently engraved on my memory.

Little Vincent spent that summer getting stuck. He put his head through the vertical spindles of the banister and had to be doused in olive oil to get his ears out.

He got his thumb stuck in the opening between a door and the jamb, and our efforts to free him, either easing the door more open or closed, both seemed to make it worse. Olive oil was involved in that rescue as well.

One afternoon when I was sitting next to him in the back seat on a long drive, he announced he had to pee. Not wanting to stop, Marthe passed him an empty wine bottle. I intercepted the bottle on its way to him and asked if, with his history, this was really wise.

My greatest challenge was that Marthe informed me I must use the familiar "tutoi" form of all verbs with the children, and with her and Alain as well, now that I was a part of the family. Ten years of school French had taught me remarkably little, certainly not the familiar form of any verb. So with the children teaching me, I embarked on changing the ending of every verb in every sentence. It gave me a terrific headache.

At first I thought in English and spoke haltingly in French, understanding only a few words of every rapidly spoken sentence. Then, as English grew more distant, although I still spoke haltingly, I understood more words. But I stopped thinking in any language. My brain felt hollow, filled only with fog. That period of time made my brain itch deep inside where I couldn't scratch. Gradually, I began to think in brief French phrases. Eventually, I even dreamed in French.

My accent gradually improved as well. Most people still knew I was American, but one man guessed I was Swiss. I remember him with great affection.

Before spending that first summer in France, my difficulty with verb tenses caused me to be regularly tutored after classes were finished for the day at Concord Academy. While everyone else was outside in the sunshine, I practiced irregular French verbs with Mlle. Bilinska two afternoons a week. She drilled me on tenses while she sat at her desk eating malted milk balls. No amount of my staring at them persuaded her to offer one to me.

When I returned to Concord for my senior year, few people knew or cared what I had been doing with my summer. I had a new French teacher, Mme. Miller, who was less authoritarian than Mlle. Bilinska.

We were all working quietly at our desks one autumn afternoon while Mme. Miller helped one student with her essay. I overheard the student asking what the French word for "a medical shot" was. Mme. Miller paused and answered, "That's hypodermique, I believe."

Being a member of a French doctor's family, I knew that one. "Piqûre," I offered.

"What?"

"The word for shot in French is piqûre."

"Oh," said Mme. Miller, then after a brief pause, "What's the gender?"

"La piqûre," I supplied. Having learned the word in France, I realized that I automatically knew its gender. Pierre would have been so proud of me.

There aren't many moments in my life that I consider pure triumph. That was one of them.

I also aced the oral portion of the French achievement test that came later in the year. I think I got 798 out of 800. I wonder what I got wrong. The French Department began to look at me with awe. This was a welcome change from the way the Chemistry Department looked at me.

That first summer, though, back when I was experiencing a world similar to two-year-old Vincent's, he and I spoke just about the same amount of French.

One day, Marthe sent me to the village store to buy a "bocoldolif." I knew my way to the store. I'd been there almost every day with one member of the family or another. I knew to smile and say, "Bonjour Mesdames, Messieurs" when I entered, and "Au revoir Mesdames, Messieurs" when I left. However, this day, no family member was free to accompany me. I would have settled gladly for Vincent, but he was busy having his afternoon nap.

I walked to the store repeating "bocoldolif" over and over, because I had no idea what it meant. No one was more surprised than I when, upon saying the magic words, I was presented with a smile and a jar of olives. Language is a miracle.

The Cornetets soon grew accustomed to my foreign ways. Marthe did her best to accommodate me, serving me Coca Cola with every meal, as the village tap water had me rushing to the toilet. She and I smoked Kool cigarettes and L&Ms respectively at the end of each long day, discussing anything and everything, and agreeing about life in general. There was such a difference in our relative status, she a married mother of four and I a high school junior, that it took several decades for me to realize how young she was. She was only twenty-nine that first summer.

French people other than my family saw me as a curiosity, and grilled me with questions; 1962 was a difficult time to be an American abroad. The newspapers were filled with photos of American police and their dogs attacking black citizens who were trying to vote, or go to school, or sit at a lunch counter. High-powered water hoses knocked crowds of black Americans off their feet, while German Shepherds bared their fangs and strained at their leashes.

How was I supposed to explain that?

"Well," I said slowly, "my nation has lost its collective mind. There is no explanation for what is happening. It is cruel and wrong."

Disappointed, perhaps, that I wasn't going to explain or defend my countrymen, the questioners would usually back off. They told me that my country was filled with abattoirs et gangstaires—slaughterhouses and gangsters. When a visitor to the Cornetet house asked what my house in America was like, I pointed to a photo of Versailles in the magazine open on my lap, and said, "Just like that." What's the point of being viewed as an ugly American if you don't work it?

Marthe remained a friend all her life. Scared of flying, she never came to America, but I visited her periodically in France. Paul and I went three times just in the past five years, and sat around huge tables with all the Cornetets: Marthe, the new "man in her life" Remo, Martine, Pierre, Veronique (who came all the way from Albi in southern France), and Vincent. They came with their spouses if they had them, and their children if those were free. We ate, and laughed, and reminisced.

In the summer of 2014, Adèle came to us for five weeks to improve her English. She is Vincent's daughter.

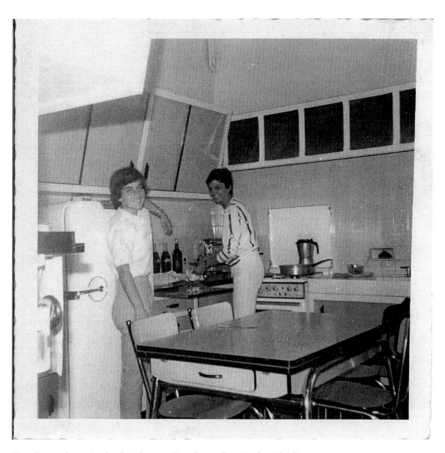

Marthe and me in the kitchen at Jonchery Sur Vesle, 1962

Part III

College, and Viet Nam

Paul

My first class at Stanford was Western Civilization. It met at seven in the morning in the living room of the freshman boys' residence, Wilbur Hall. My freshman women's dorm, Roble, was across campus, so it took a brisk bike ride through the chill or the rain to get there.

Paul, on the other hand, lived in Wilbur and only had to come down one flight of stairs to reach this first class of the morning. I realize now that this meant I was awake and he wasn't.

I sat on an upholstered chair in that living room, with my crisp spiral binder and my newly sharpened pencil, and waited for college to begin. There were about twenty freshmen in that class, half boys and half girls, and it was taught by a serious graduate student named Mr. Savage. I scanned the faces of my classmates, knowing no one and hoping to learn their names. I spent my evenings looking through the Froshbook, with its thumbnail photos of all 1,300 of us, trying to match names to the faces in my classes.

Mr. Savage tried to keep us awake by peppering us with questions about our reading of the night before. He learned our names and pounced on us unexpectedly. There was no pretense that he was going to call on the person who had a thought or wanted to answer a question. He called on the person he thought wasn't paying attention. We each got caught in his trap occasionally.

"I don't know, sir. Could you repeat the question, sir?"

But Mr. Savage never called on the pale, quiet boy who often came late, and who, one memorable morning, entered the room in his red and white striped pajamas, having forgotten the class entirely and simply wanting to cross the living room to get to the kitchen. That entry and hasty departure caused a wave of laughter, and when I got back to my room, I scanned the Froshbook until I found that face: Paul de Blank.

It wasn't until the end of the autumn quarter, just before we disbanded for Christmas, that Mr. Savage directed a question at Paul de Blank.

"So tell me, Mr. de Blank, what distinguished the so-called Dark Ages from the period just preceding it?"

Paul looked startled. No one had told him that the comfortable rules of the game, where everyone was called on but him, had suddenly changed.

"Uh, it was called Dark because it came after the decline of the Roman Empire."

"Yes," said Mr. Savage, turning the spotlight of his gaze to the next victim.

I sat there stunned. I now understood the reason why Paul had never been asked a question until now. It was not, as I had assumed, because he was mildly retarded, but because he couldn't speak English. He had a very thick northern European accent. It wasn't French, it wasn't quite German. What the hell was it?

When I returned to Stanford the next year, I was even more determined to meet people, preferably men. I had consulted Jane, whose profound advice on picking men was to go for the man who knew to wear dark socks with dark trousers. She also told me to join everything I could find. So I signed up for a weekend ski trip to Reno in late January.

I got on the rented bus with everyone else for the long ride to Squaw Valley. I skied with my friend Sue Carter during the day, somehow managing not to break either leg, and went to the mixer that evening. The dance was held in a crowded living room of the lodge, with records and a DJ, and lots of nonalcoholic punch.

A boy I didn't know asked me to dance. We went out on the floor to the new album *Introducing ... The Beatles*. Our dance stretched through several songs, and we didn't know how to get out of this. No one else cut in to ask me to dance, the nameless boy seemed unable to think of a reason to move on. I seemed unable to encourage him to do so. Finally, with the finesse of a freshman, he suggested that I must be thirsty and he would fetch me a cup of punch. I embraced this idea enthusiastically, and told him I would return to a chair. I admired his initiative. We both knew we would never see each other again.

I sat in my chair at the edge of the dance floor thinking this was ridiculous. Here were all these people, and I wanted to meet people, and I was doing nothing. So when a familiar face passed my chair, I put out my foot and tripped him. He stumbled slightly but didn't fall.

"Ah, aren't you Paul de Blank?" I asked, steadying him. "I believe you were in my Western Civ last year."

"I was? I mean, yes, of course. I've just forgotten your name."

"Laura Kennedy."

"Of course. I remember now. Would you like to dance?"

We moved out onto the floor and yelled bits of conversation at each other over the music.

"Where are you from?" I asked.

"You know where I'm from."

"No, actually I have no idea."

"Guess,"

"Belgium?"

"God no! I'm from Holland."

"Your English is getting better."

"Thanks."

A riveting conversation. Definitely the stuff that predicts compatibility and a lifetime spent together.

I was determined not to dance so long with Paul that we would have that same awkward parting that I'd had with my last partner, so I quit while I was ahead.

"Thank you for the dance, Paul. I'm going back to my room now, as I have to get up early in the morning."

"I'll walk you back."

Paul walked me out of the dance, along the icy outdoor walkway that led to the hotel rooms, and up to my door. I thanked him again for the dance, and he said he hoped he'd see me back on campus.

As he walked away, I noted dark socks with dark trousers, and I smiled.

Our Chicano Revolutionary

Paul and I married in September of 1967, after graduation from Stanford and a summer working to save some money. We moved into a small rose-covered cottage in Palo Alto, so Paul could get his master's degree in thermodynamics. I had trouble finding a job. I'd been rejected at all my job hunting attempts on campus.

In our tiny rented house each evening, sitting at our wedding-present-new folding table with matching folding chairs, and eating a dinner of spaghetti and frozen peas, Paul would try to rebuild my confidence after my day of job hunting.

"No, no, your diploma isn't completely worthless," he said. "It's because you're married. They see the ring on your finger and decide they'll hold out for a single girl."

"Thanks, that's kind," I said, "but we both know that they're holding out for a girl with bigger boobs."

So I expanded my job search from campus to Palo Alto, and got a job at Spiro's Sporting Goods Store. Spiro's doesn't exist any longer—Manuel and I have looked for it—but it used to be in a strip mall called Town and Country Shopping Center. It sold every piece of athletic equipment imaginable and all the clothes to go with them.

On that first day of work, I stood in my section of the store, refolding sweaters and hanging up tennis skirts, when a disembodied voice floated in through the open door of the stock room.

"Oh, a new girl.... Hi, little white girl!"

There were no customers in my department, so I followed the voice through the open door. There, in the stockroom, looking remarkably like the Cheshire Cat, stood Manuel. He was a couple of years older than I was, maybe twenty-three, with black hair brushed back, a thick black mustache, and deep chocolate eyes. He smelled faintly of soap and aftershave, and except that I was newly married, I fell in love at first sight.

The stock room was Manuel's kingdom. He had arranged it with deep niches and towering walls of boxes. Dust motes floated in the light of the only window. There was a counter meant for reboxing returned items. It made a good place for me to sit and talk with Manuel.

Manuel taught me that his name was Manuel, not Manny.

"Manuel translates to 'walks with God,'" he explained. "Manny means 'fell down, dropped God's hand, and was left behind.' And also," he continued, "I am not Hispanic, or Mexican-American, I am *Chicano*. Don't forget it."

California in 1967 was a time and place of love, drugs, and revolution, and Manuel was a revolutionary. He had no patience for political hypocrisy or stupidity. On slow afternoons, I sat on the storeroom counter watching Manuel work, listening to his political views. "I am a much better debater than the typical candidate," he stated, his eyes flashing. "However, they never let a communist participate, especially the brown ones."

As a first step to the overthrow of the social order, he suggested, with a piratical gleam in his eye, that he and I go out to steal hubcaps, or else take a shovel with us at night to dig up houseplants from other people's gardens to plant at my house. I declined politely. However, when the revolution erupted into pitched battles in the streets, I wanted a man with such initiative to let me and Paul join him behind the barricades. And in case capitalism and white privilege triumphed, we'd do the same for him.

It was occasionally difficult to remember that I was married. That change in my status had occurred only a month before. There was another salesgirl in my department named Julie, even younger than I was, and not married. We were kicking our heels one quiet afternoon, talking about life and sex, and Manuel's voice came from the stock room. "I love to hear a virgin discussing sex!" I knew that in the stockroom, Manuel's mustache was quivering with laughter.

Julie and I were quiet for a minute, trying to think of an adequate response to this crushing remark, and then I remembered that I was married now, and didn't even have to pretend to be a virgin. He couldn't have been talking to me. My chest swelled with pride.

I invited Manuel home and introduced him to Paul. We had dinner, smoked pot, and watched television. The two men laughed together over the pundits on the evening news, reaching simultaneously for the plate of chocolate chip cookies.

I took this photo of Manuel and Paul in the spring, as the three of us walked in Haight-Ashbury. Manuel is striding along, dark and handsome, comfortable in his own skin, and Paul, soon to go to Viet Nam, is in his brand new flowered Nehru jacket, with his short military haircut and black plastic, military-issue glasses—a moment of friendship, frozen in time. Manuel's comment when he saw the photo was, "There's such a contrast between Paul's military head and his hippie chest that it looks as though someone has been playing paper dolls with him."

Manuel and Paul, Haight-Ashbury, 1968

Manuel was single and so was our co-worker, young Julie. Wiser than I, he asked her to go out to lunch with him. He'd never asked me to lunch. I watched them leave the store—Julie was far too young and shallow for Manuel. She didn't have my deep appreciation for his radical politics and his long thick eyelashes. It wasn't easy for me, wanting everything all at the same time. I was sitting on one of my display tables, flattening a pile of freshly folded sweaters, when they returned. I stared down at my hands in my lap, feeling sorry for myself—an old woman, off the market and on the shelf. Manuel, protective of me always, walked softly behind me, and pushing my hair to one side, kissed the nape of my neck.

*   *   *   *

Manuel is dying now, slowly and elegantly, only one lung left. He reminds me of this fact each time we speak on the telephone. He tells me I should feel terrible about this and should write and call him more often … and send chocolate chip cookies. He is possibly happier than he has ever been.

I am connected to him by a thick cable from my heart to his, each strand made from a memory. Our relationship was forged by one year of working together in Spiro's Sporting Goods Store, followed by forty-six years of correspondence. I always send my love to his wife Lucy, and he sends his love to Paul.

Email from Manuel to me upon his reading the first draft of this essay:

> Attached is corrected copy. Just a couple of grammatical corrections. As always your writing flows until it ebbs, then quietly and warmly it flows once again. The first part (2-3) paragraphs help set the tone and offer insight into your personality at the time, but it takes you too long to get to me. The result is that you fail to add more about me. I loved it and I love you all over again.
>
> Me

Manuel, 1997

Florence Nightingale and Me
at Reynolds Army Hospital

In June, when Paul finished his master's degree, he and I said goodbye to Manuel, packed up our puppy, and left Palo Alto for Paul's job in the Army. He had been in ROTC (Reserve Officer Training Corps) throughout college in order to cement his citizenship. Since his father was Dutch and his mother was American, both countries claimed him. In the late 1960s, Holland had a military draft, and if Paul had returned on a long visit to his parents he would have been drafted there. The United States, at that time, said that if anyone served in the military of a foreign country, he lost his American citizenship. So to stabilize his American citizenship and to do his duty by his country, Paul knew he would enter the Army. Since he was an officer, however junior, I was able to go with him.

The Army had waited, none too patiently, through Paul's master's degree, and now it pounced, ready to train him and send him to Viet Nam.

In 1968, his first assignment was to basic artillery training at Ft. Sill in Lawton, Oklahoma. My memories of places are intertwined with the sense of who I was when I was there. At Ft. Sill, I was a twenty-two-year-old Red Cross volunteer at Reynolds Army Hospital.

Lawton is in the heart of the Bible Belt. I'd never lived in the South. In fact, my general naiveté was so extensive that geography was the least of my problems. Base housing wasn't available, so we set off in our Volkswagen Beetle with a list of possible apartments we'd gotten from the housing bulletin board. We found a small, dusty apartment and negotiated with the landlady, who had an alarming number of pictures of Jesus on her walls. That is to say, I should have been alarmed, but at the time I didn't understand the culture that went with the geography.

Paul and I moved in with our two pots and pans and our small dog, Brownie, to join the millions of cockroaches already living there.

One month later, our landlady approached us and told us she would have to ask us to leave. "I didn't know you had a dog," she said. "I don't allow dogs."

This was confusing, as she had seen Brownie when we

interviewed, and again when we signed the lease. Paul surmised that we were no longer suitable tenants because we had declined her invitation to accompany her to all-day church services. Or perhaps she had seen the beer in our refrigerator, or the absence of photos of Jesus on our dresser. I figured she had found someone who was willing to pay more.

Paul and I moved into another cockroach-infested apartment and got on with our lives.

Usually Paul was busy in basic artillery training, learning to aim and fire the self-propelled guns, so I looked around for something to do. We were only going to be at Ft. Sill for six months, so a paid job was unlikely. I signed up with the Red Cross to be trained as a nurse's aide at Reynolds Army Hospital.

That choice may have been influenced by the romance novels of my childhood, many of them about women nursing men back to health, and saving them from their demons. The children's section of my town library was stocked with books on Florence Nightingale, *Sue Barton: Student Nurse*, and *Cherry Ames: Army Nurse*. I had read them all.

Two elderly women, whose names I have forgotten, taught the Red Cross nursing class in the basement of the hospital. I will call them The Skinny One with Blue Hair and The Plump One with Purple Hair. These women diligently taught a group of six of us how to take temperatures, pulse, and respiration; how to give bed baths (an intriguing idea); and how to change bed pans, wash down units, and change the sheets of a bed with the patient still in it.

Our training also covered emergency first aid, in case of a natural or military disaster.

"Now, imagine you are in a disaster. Who can tell me how you would sterilize a wound without any regular medical supplies?" asked The Skinny One with Blue Hair.

I raised my hand proudly, "We could use bourbon to sterilize the wounds, ma'am."

Blue Hair and Purple Hair looked at each other in silence for a long minute. Purple Hair turned to me and said with gentle sadness, "In a disaster, that would be a terrible waste of the bourbon."

When I started work at the hospital, I reported to a busy nurse, who told me to go to Room 274 to see what the man in Bed B wanted. The boy/man in Bed B was cold and wanted a blanket. His name was Tony, and he looked even younger than I was.

Finding an extra blanket in that hospital was surprisingly difficult.

There were none in the storeroom, but by walking in and out of every room, I eventually found one two floors down.

"Thanks," said Tony, as I shook the blanket over him, thus fulfilling one of my *Cherry Ames, Army Nurse* dreams. It's a shame he didn't seem feverish, or I could have stroked his brow.

"Wounded in 'Nam," he mentioned briefly. "It doesn't hurt so much anymore. Soon I'll be well enough to rejoin my unit."

A nurse heard our conversation, and looked down at Tony's chart on the foot of the bed, reading out loud, "Car accident, drunk driving, Lawton, Oklahoma."

Tony and I looked at each other, recognizing kindred spirits.

*   *   *   *

In between emptying bedpans, and scrubbing down each metal bed frame and plastic-covered mattress when a patient left, I met more patients.

I was assigned to read to the man in Room 236. He was sitting up in bed, doing nothing, and had a broad bandage across his eyes. While he was still unaware of my presence, I studied him from across the room. My God, he was handsome.

It hadn't yet occurred to me that Lawton was a long way from Viet Nam, and the likelihood that these soldiers were wounded on the front lines was slim. But after my experience with Tony, I did glance at this soldier's chart at the foot of his bed and saw that his name was Jim and he had hit a deer with his car, and when it came in through his windshield, shards of glass had lacerated his eyes.

"What would you like me to read to you?" I asked.

"My letters, please," Jim said, his voice soft and low. "I've wanted to know the news from home, but I'm not allowed to raise my bandage."

I read letter after letter, from sisters, brothers, mother, and girlfriend. They were filled with warmth and family news. "The crops are almost in. Let's hope this weather holds."

A nurse came in and said, "My, don't you two just make a picture! Pretty young girl reading to a handsome soldier. Do you know how lucky you are, soldier?"

"Yes," he replied, "I peeked."

*   *   *   *

"When you're finished here, you can go to Room 215 and take the patient in Bed C to X-ray." A nurse had found me emptying my bowl of sudsy water and hauling the mattress back onto a bed.

Room 215, when I found it, seemed full of people and merriment. Not only were all the beds full, a couple of orderlies leaned against the walls, joking around with the patients. My patient sat on the edge of bed C, staring grimly at the wheelchair he was supposed to get into.

"Get your slippers on, man," said the orderly, who made no effort to help. "Don't keep a lady waiting."

My patient from bed C was black, but the undertones of his skin were greenish/gray. He eased a foot out toward the slipper, but as he tried to slide his foot into it, it slipped farther away.

"Come on, man, hurry it up," said the white orderly, who looked first at the slipper that was clearly out of reach and then, with a grin, at the other men in the room.

I pushed past the orderlies and retrieved the two slippers, putting them firmly on bed C's feet. His name was William, and he was here for a gunshot wound. While the others simply watched, I maneuvered the wheelchair to his bedside, and he managed to get himself from bed to chair by using his arms. He was too tall for me, and it was clear we weren't going to get any help from those orderlies.

William and I talked as I wheeled him through the halls to the elevator, and then down two floors, and through more hallways, following the signs for X-ray.

"I went to Lawton with two buddies, both white guys," he said in answer to my question of what had happened. "We were just walking down the street, and a panhandler asked us for a handout. We all refused, and when we walked away, he shot me in the back."

I waited in the hall while William got his X-rays, ready to take him back to bed. An orderly wheeled him out to me, and for some reason, there were now bits of lint in William's hair. As we waited for the elevator, I gently picked out bits of fluff and dropped them on the floor. I'd never touched a black man's hair before.

When I'd done, William turned his face toward me, and said softly, "Thank you."

*   *   *   *

Disappointingly, I wasn't usually asked to give bed baths to the men, only the women. Then one day, a nurse told me to bathe the retired General in Room 281. He had just had open heart surgery and wasn't allowed up yet. I entered his room with my bath supplies, cheerfully explaining what I was about to do to him. In my eyes, the General seemed about 104 years old, withered and cranky. It never occurred to me then that he might find it humiliating to have a twenty-two-year-old girl assigned to bathe him, clearly signifying that, in the eyes of the nurses, he was no longer a man at all.

I washed his face and hands, and then moved on to his arms and legs as I had been taught. I would move each limb out from under the covers, and then return it to the warmth before removing the next one. I had been taught that a bed bath ended with handing the washcloth to the patient with instructions to reach beneath the covers and wash his or her own private parts.

The General, however, had apparently taken as much of this shilly-shallying as he could stand. When I handed him the washcloth, he said, "Oh for God's sake, woman, just get on with it," and threw the covers off himself. His naked body was an impressive sight, from his skinny arms and legs, to the livid, purple scar that carved him in two from just below his throat to just above his pubic hair.

"Yes, General," I said, thinking as I bathed him, that it was a damn good thing I was already married, or this might have put me off men forever.

*   *   *   *

Another day, a nurse sent me to Room 243, a single room, telling me that a young soldier had had a brain aneurism burst, and that although he was still alive, he was, in truth, dead. He would never regain consciousness, and his family had been called. They were coming from California to say goodbye.

I don't remember why I was sent to his room, perhaps for temperature, pulse, and respiration, but more probably because the nurse felt someone should be with him. His name was Joshua, and when I arrived in his room, he seemed to be asleep.

Joshua was beautiful, slim and lightly tanned, his face relaxed and grave. He lay on the bed, unnervingly still, with the crisp white sheets pulled up to just below his bare shoulders. There were no tubes in him, and he breathed on his own. However, there was not a single wrinkle in the sheets to suggest that he had moved of his own volition since he had been put in that bed.

I entered the TPR information on his chart, talking to him all the while about the summer thunderstorm raging just outside the hermetically sealed windows, and that his family would be here soon. It seemed crueler to leave this unconscious man alone than any of the conscious ones in the other rooms.

I felt shy of this man. If he had been healthy, his beauty would have put him out of my league. His unconsciousness seemed like self-possession, removing human frailty. I felt I needed an excuse to stay there, so I straightened his already tidy room, filling the empty water glass from the pitcher, and lining the tissue box up with the edge of the table. His family will need these, I thought. When there was nothing left to be done, I pulled up a straight-backed chair and sat down beside him.

Joshua and I existed in a pocket of suspended time, between the robust health of yesterday and the finality of tomorrow. His room was warm and dry compared to the rain on the windows.

"My God, you're beautiful," I told him. "What happened to you is wrong. It shocks me. How can you be dying when you weren't attacked by warfare, or accident, or racism, or even by old age. How can you be gone?"

I was one strong young animal looking at another. His skin was still rosy, and his eyelashes rested in a thick fringe on his cheeks. I leaned down, close to his shoulder, and gently lifted the top of the sheet six inches, to glance under it along the length of his bare body. I wanted to see if his body was as beautiful as his face.

It was. He was Apollo, sleeping.

"You're beautiful, all of you," I told him. "Goodbye, Joshua."

It's a good thing my time in Lawton was almost finished. I wasn't cut out to be an Army nurse, or a redeemer of men.

Goodbye for Now

Basic artillery training could not last forever. But the airplane flight to Paul's embarkation point at San Francisco seemed to. The upholstery itched the back of my legs, and I was filled with a tightly controlled energy that made me want to scream against the restriction of my seatbelt. I shoved the *Ladies Home Journal* into my backpack, tired of reading the same sentence over and over. Beside me, Paul read his book, though I hadn't seen him turn a page in hours. We rode in silence. What could we say?

"Save me, I am being torn to shreds," or "I'm sure everything will be all right."

I leaned toward the window for a moment. There was nothing to see but painfully harsh sunshine, blue sky, and a field of white clouds. I couldn't see the earth. I wasn't lost. Lost would have been good if it meant no one could find us. No, the plane was taking us to San Francisco. I was just untethered. I straightened in my seat, leaning back toward Paul, and pressed my arm, from shoulder to elbow, against his. His warmth spread through me.

As the plane descended through the clouds, I saw the sharp edge where the land met the sea. The Pacific was a barrier I was not allowed to follow Paul across. This was as far west as I could go. He would continue in a troop transport to Viet Nam.

We gathered our possessions and filed off the plane. I reached for Paul. He shifted his book to his right hand and squeezed my hand with his left. He looked pretty sharp in his dress greens. We had polished his shoes that morning before leaving for the airport, and given his 2nd Lieutenant bars a final buffing. Tomorrow, he would leave the greens with me, and from then on dress only in fatigues, nothing polished. His insignia would be made of black cloth, and his boots would be dull. Nothing should shine. Nothing should glint in the sun.

We had one night left. The next day he would take a flight early in the morning, and later in the day I would fly back to Chicago. Thank God it would be early. I didn't know how much more goodbye I could bear.

Paul pulled his big green duffel bag off the carousel and hoisted it on his back. I had my clothes for the night in my backpack. We had reserved a room in a motel near the airport: it was too far to walk, and the motel was too cheap to have a shuttle bus, so we took a cab. Money spent on a cab meant less for dinner. Night closed in quickly, and we couldn't see much of the motel as we checked in. The receptionist had the lyrical accent of India, and there was a smell of curry coming from the back room.

Paul and I walked along the broken sidewalk to the door of our room, unlocked it and turned on the light. A 40-watt ceiling bulb gave enough light to find the furniture, and nothing more. There was a queen size bed, a dresser, and a television set with rabbit ears. We put our bags down in the corner and sat next to each other on the bed.

"OK," Paul said, "it's 7:30. We ought to find some dinner."

"Yes," I agreed, knowing that my stomach didn't want food, but at least it was something to do, something normal.

Neon lights from the diner nearby made the outdoors seem brighter than our room. We walked across the parking lot and entered the restaurant, wood paneling on the walls and the smell of cigarette smoke trapped in the furniture. The click of pool balls came from the back of the room, and a basketball game played on the TV mounted over the bar.

We ordered. We ate. I couldn't taste it. We talked a bit, but only about my future, not his. How would the dog and cat like moving with me to my parents' home? What sort of job would I look for once I'd settled? Somehow dinner passed. We paid from our careful hoard of cash, then walked slowly, hand in hand, back to our room.

"It's 8:30," I said. "Do you want to watch TV or go to bed?"

"Both, I guess," he replied.

The TV received only three channels, two of them filled with visual static, so we took the only choice we had, and watched the end of the basketball game that had been playing in the diner. Neither of us knew or cared about basketball, but we pulled back the nylon bedspread, got between the gray, pilled sheets, and watched it anyway. Gradually, we turned to each other and sank down in the bed. We held each other and loved each other. It was a strange lovemaking, distracted, exhausted, and desperate.

"I love you," I told him.

"And I love you," he replied.

We lay still, both staring at the shifting pattern of neon lights coming through a chink in the curtains onto the ceiling. I commanded my breathing into slow deep waves, hiding in the dark and the silence, pretending to sleep. I felt small movements from Paul beside me and knew that he too was awake. Sleep would have been a blessing, but it wasn't going to come. Nothing to do now but wait, fill the remaining time with thought. I wondered what a year without Paul would be like, and what if it wasn't a year, but forever.

My mind shied away from thoughts of Paul and bullets in the humid jungle. I moved my body until it touched his down our length, and wished I could go with him. What if he got lonely, or was scared, or hurt?

I waited for the night to pass.

The Year of Viet Nam

After Paul had left for Viet Nam in August, 1969, and the dog, cat, and I had moved in with my parents in Lake Forest, we all had a lot of adjusting to do. I have more sympathy for my parents now than I did then. I felt as though I were age twenty-three going on six in their house. Now I see that having a grown, worried daughter return home couldn't have been easy.

I didn't move into my childhood bedroom, but into the guest room, instead, harboring the vague hope that I could cling to the edge of adulthood and not drown in parental concern and nurturing.

I knew that I needed something to do. I hadn't lived full time in this home since I went away to boarding school at fourteen. I went with Mother to a woman who painted needlepoint pictures on open-weave canvas, and together we chose a pattern for a five foot by seven foot rug that, like Penelope's tapestry, I would sew while my husband was away at the wars. Visiting Mother's friends with her during the day and sewing in front of the television at night lasted about two weeks. I knew I was going mad.

Looking around for work, I found a volunteer job in the daycare center in the church basement across the street. I caught every cold the children had, and was almost as interested in this job as I had been in needlepoint. One of the students was a little girl from Haiti, and the school needed to write her monolingual French-speaking parents a letter. I offered to write it.

Everyone was quite pleased with me, and somehow the word spread to someone in the public school system, where there was a need for a teacher of English as a Second Language in nearby Waukegan. The school system knew that I would leave in a year, when my husband returned from Viet Nam, God willing, but they were desperate, so they hired me.

I was an itinerant teacher, teaching ESL at three different schools in the daytime and to adults in the same classrooms in the evenings. I had no training, but worked under a competent girl of my own age who had actually been trained to be a teacher. There were no workbooks or materials for teaching ESL that we knew of, so we made up our own on the mimeograph machine. It was a lot of fun.

My mother was afraid of my driving alone back and forth to Waukegan at night, and was about to forbid it. If she had, what would we all have done? Fortunately, my father intervened and said he would take responsibility for my safety. I don't think any of us knew what that meant. Would he take the brunt of Mother's wrath if anything happened to me? He demonstrated his responsibility by being outside walking my dog every night when I got home around 10 PM. Some of those nights were very cold indeed.

I wrote to Paul every other day, and waited by the mailbox for his infrequent replies. During the six-week period that included Thanksgiving, his birthday, Christmas, New Year's, and my birthday, I heard nothing at all. At night, I lay in bed trying not to imagine the sounds of rifle fire and artillery shells exploding. Whenever my mind supplied pictures of blood and the sound of screams, I forcibly switched my mental channel to imagine his disgust at eating C rations, and his laughter with his friends about what might be in them.

Because of his background in mathematics and engineering, Paul was assigned to be Fire Control Officer. He calculated azimuth, elevation, and charge for the great cannons. "I hope to make the bombardments as accurate as humanly possible, to confine war to the combatants," he wrote.

One evening, my parents went to a fancy dinner party in Chicago. I was reading in the living room when they got home. I looked up and saw that my father was spluttering with outrage. Recent newspapers had reported that Sweden had come out against the Viet Nam war, and the hosts of the dinner party had seated my father at the same table as the Swedish Consul. My father refused to sit with him. The host hurriedly rearranged the place cards

I appreciated Father's fierce loyalty, but as neither Paul nor I were much in favor of the Viet Nam war, it was hard to know exactly what to say. I wrote it all to Paul in a letter, and eventually got back his reply.

"Please thank your father for defending me so strongly with the Swedish Consul," he said, "but it isn't necessary. If I am not over here in the mud fighting for freedom of speech, what am I fighting for?"

Soldiers were sent to the Viet Nam war for twelve months, and then their tour was over, and somewhere between the beginning and the end, the Red Cross arranged for the soldier, and his wife if he had one, to have a week of Rest and Recuperation in Hawaii or Japan. R and R had to be taken when a soldier still had at least two months of combat duty left. I waited and waited for word from Paul that we could meet somewhere. With time running out, and Paul only saying he had asked his commanding officer for R and R, nothing more he could do, my father once again stepped forward. I don't know whom he knew at the Red Cross or what he said to them, but he left for work looking determined, and he came home looking pleased. A few days later, I received my official notification that I could meet Paul in Hawaii for a week in April.

Paul using a theodolite to orient the six howitzers of the battery, 1970

I let the school know the days I would need off, and announced to my child and adult classes that I would be gone for a week and why. The lovely adult students got together, in all their different languages, and secretly took up a collection to give me a present. They gathered around me on my last night and waited for me to unwrap the bright paper. Inside the box was a lacy and transparent negligee with a matching and equally transparent dressing gown. I blushed hotly and thanked them, stopping myself just short of holding the gown up against myself. I would have to face these people again in a week, and I hated to imagine what they would be thinking about as I stood at the front of the class reviewing verb tenses.

I packed some of Paul's clothes with mine, so he'd have something to wear in Hawaii other than jungle fatigues. We met in Honolulu, and a day later moved on to Kauai. He seemed to be all knees and elbows, down to 135 pounds.

We didn't talk about the war. It was so good to see him that I would have happily spent the week just staring.

In Kauai, we had a hotel room on the beach. The waves lapped at the shore just twenty paces from our door, and palm trees framed the view. There must have been other people at the hotel, but I don't remember a single one. We spent long lazy mornings on our lanai, sipping coffee and reading the newspapers. Then we'd go for a swim, and laugh at each other's attempts to master the hotel's surfboards on the gentle waves outside our door. We'd swing in the hammock hung between the palm trees, then eat a long lingering dinner, and go back to bed.

This happy and mindless interlude lasted until the morning when Paul picked up the newspaper and announced, in a voice that shook with horror, the date on its heading. "April 23rd!" Thrown off by the day it had taken us to reach Kauai, we'd thought our last day would be tomorrow. "My God, I have to report back to duty at the Honolulu airport in three hours!"

We dressed, threw clothes into my suitcase and his duffle bag, called a taxi, paid the hotel bill, and rushed to the Kauai airport for a plane to Honolulu, all in the space of fifteen minutes. Paul told me about the punishment for AWOL in wartime, and although I didn't really believe they would shoot him, I was panicked, too.

In many ways that fright and turmoil made the parting easier. We didn't have time to linger or imagine or grieve. We ran.

Still panting, we reached the gate from which he would proceed to the troop transport embarking for Tan Son Nhut Airbase in Saigon, only minutes to spare. We held each other, promised to write, told each other it wouldn't be much longer now before he'd be home for good, and said goodbye. Paul lined up with the other men and boarded a bus to his plane.

I watched and waved until the bus was out of sight, then slowly turned and walked to my plane for the long flight back to Illinois.

By the time my plane was over the Pacific, the numbness had worn off. I felt the full weight of the pain. I put my face in my hands and wept.

I felt a tap on my shoulder and lifted my sodden, tear-streaked face to a white-haired woman leaning over me.

"Excuse me, dear, but if you're not going to watch the movie, would you mind trading seats with me. Your seat has a much better view of the screen."

Our first dinner together in Hawaii, 1971

Weird as she was, she had a point. I couldn't see the screen through my swollen eyes, so I exchanged seats with her.

I returned to my thoughts of Paul eating mysterious C rations with his friends, and waiting.

Part IV

Adult Life

A Driveway Conversation

"I've been married to your mother longer than I haven't been married to her," my father said, driving me home from a Saturday errand to the hardware store.

I was vacationing with my parents on Cape Cod. Paul had returned from Viet Nam, gone to law school at Columbia, and was now working at a law firm in Hartford, Connecticut, where we were raising four-year-old Bas and one-year-old Peter.

I did the math in my head and said, "You married at thirty-four, so this is your thirty-fifth anniversary coming up. That must seem very strange—to have been with someone longer than you haven't."

My father pulled the car up to the garage but made no move to turn off the engine or get out. "Yes, it is strange—a choice creates an entire life—a responsibility. When I die," he continued, not looking at me but straight ahead, "you will have to look after your mother."

"Sure, Dad," I replied. Bas was getting restless in his car seat, although Peter was fast asleep. I reached for the door handle, ready to end this conversation. I wondered whether he had been told he was dying, but for all I knew he was fine. Had he had this conversation with Jane too? Was this to be a joint responsibility? Did Mother know that she was getting passed to me? I was twenty-nine and didn't want to figure out the details of this distant problem now. Life would keep on going as it always had.

I got the kids out of the car, and we went together into the house.

Two years later, on a warm April night, my father collapsed in the bathroom of my parents' home in Lake Forest, with what turned out to be a combination of heart attack and stroke. The paramedics rushed him to the hospital.

Paul and I and the kids were living in Phoenix when Mother called to tell me.

"Your father is in the hospital," she said. "He's very bad."

As soon as I hung up, I started looking for flights to get to him. It was the end of spring break. All of Chicago seemed to be returning home from Phoenix. There were no seats to be had. I got myself waitlisted on all the flights I could, and called Mother to discuss driving or taking a train.

"No," she said, "Your father and I were there in Phoenix just a couple of weeks ago, visiting you. He can't speak, and if he opens his eyes and sees the whole family standing around his bed, he'll be sure he's dying. It's better if you don't come."

I stood by the phone and listened to her voice telling me I wasn't needed.

"Your sister is here," she said, "so I have support. I'll let you know what happens."

"Give Dad my love," was all I said.

I felt just as I had fifteen years earlier, when Mother had called me at boarding school to say that my father had testicular cancer and was going to have surgery.

"Bring me home!" I demanded. When she didn't reply, I said less confidently, "Please get me a flight. I want to come home."

"No," she said after a pause. "I have Jane here, so I have support. Jane can take time off from college more easily than you can. You can help me most by staying put."

It seemed selfish to say I wasn't worried about supporting her, or even Dad, but supporting myself—emotional support from drowning. So I said nothing.

After his stroke, my father lasted two days in the hospital, and then I got another call from Mother saying he was dead. She was holding herself together. "A memorial service will be planned and I'll need you to take whatever flight you can. We can schedule it out a week or two, so let me know what you can get."

I said goodbye to her and walked outside to the backyard. The hot April morning was gray, without a breeze. The trees stood solidly in the earth: the mulberry, the evergreen pear, palms, and mock orange. I walked to each, touching its bark, and saying, "My father is dead." I said it until I believed it.

Later that night, lying next to Paul, I couldn't sleep, and I couldn't stay still, either. I wanted a cigarette. I hadn't smoked in years, but this seemed like a good night to take it up again. I slipped out of bed and drove to Denny's, the closest twenty-four-hour restaurant with a cigarette machine. A sleepy waitress continually refilled my iced tea glass while I sat in a booth smoking cigarettes until three in the morning. I thanked my father for everything I had probably failed to thank him for when he was alive.

Thank you, Dad, for taking me to the train one afternoon when I was a teenager traveling somewhere on my own. You found me a good seat and placed my suitcase in the overhead rack. I looked around and said, "Damn, I forgot my book!"

You said, "Well, it's too late now."

Thank you for running the length of the platform to the newsstand, buying me a magazine, and running back, out of breath, so that I'd have something to read on the train.

Thank you, Dad, for telling me, "You'll be the prettiest girl there," each time I left the house for dancing class or a party.

Thank you, Dad, for writing to me every single day that I was in boarding school. Back home for summer break, sitting with you on the porch, when I complained your notes were only three sentences long, the letters an inch high to fill the page, and that they gave no news, you replied, "I just want there always to be a letter for you in your mailbox."

OK, Dad. I remember our conversation in the driveway. I'll do what I can for Mom.

The Rowboat—Part Two, 1977

I loved Ben from the time I first met him that summer when I was eleven and he was forty-two. After that, we had one more summer together, twenty years of correspondence, and an occasional chance to visit. "Love, Laura," I said at the end of my letters. "Best Luck, Ben," he'd reply.

Paul handed me a letter from Ben out of the stack of mail he was sorting. The postmark was January 20, 1977. I opened it with one hand while stirring dinner with the other. The kitchen was filled with people: Paul, our small sons Bas and Peter, and Paul's brother Maurits and his wife Teresita, our houseguests. Paul and I were still living in Connecticut, and Ben and his second wife Betty lived in New Hampshire.

"Five days ago," Ben wrote, "I began to sprout a swelling under my ear along my left shoulder. It kept growing and finally I went to my local doctor. One look at me, and he's ordered me into Notre Dame Hospital in Manchester where I'm getting every test there is. Such a surprise development is OK by me but terribly hard on Betty."

Ben ended with, "You sent me a very fine letter five weeks back and I apologize for being so damn slow in answering it. I get such a real lift from all your letters—short or long—that I never want to do anything that will discourage you from writing whenever you feel like it."

I stopped stirring and read Ben's letter out loud to Paul and the others, the words ricocheting around the warm kitchen.

"What do you want to do?" Paul asked when I'd finished.

"I want to go to him," I said, turning off the stove, and moving the pot out of reach of the children. I went to sit with him at the kitchen table.

Paul looked at the kids. "What about them? I have to set out for Arizona in just a few days. The job is waiting, and I've got to start studying for the bar."

My warm-hearted sister-in-law spoke up. "Maurits and I will come back from New York and take care of your children any weekend you want."

"Oh, thank you!" I said, rising to hug her.

I left them all in the kitchen and went upstairs to use the bedroom phone. I asked information for the number of Notre Dame Hospital. The switchboard connected me to Ben's room.

"Ah, Ben, I'm sorry to hear your news. How are you feeling?"

With his Boston and Cape Cod accent, lyrical and compelling, he said, "I'm very comfortable. The hospital is taking excellent care of me. I just worry about Betty because she's without a driver's license. They took it away when she started the new psychotropic drugs. She can't get here to see me, and she worries."

My real obstacle in going to Ben was not finding babysitting for the kids, but Ben himself. I feared that he would tell me don't come, it's not necessary, don't go to so much trouble. All the excuses of a shy man.

I spotted my opportunity. "I could come up there on a weekend and bring Betty to see you."

"Yes, come," was all he said.

A few days later Paul packed the back of the small VW station wagon for his move to Phoenix. We put in the card table, two folding chairs, a sleeping bag, a pot, a pan, two plates and glasses and a few pieces of silverware. With a long kiss and a cheery wave, he set off on the drive.

About two months pregnant, I stayed behind to sell the house. I kept it as clean as two small children would allow. I put refrigerated bread dough in the oven to bake whenever I knew prospective buyers were coming to view the house, and followed Jane's suggestion of putting most of our clothes in the car in order to make the closets look bigger.

There was so much I didn't know. When would the house sell? When would the boys and I move to Arizona? How long would Ben live? I needed to get to him now, while I was still in Connecticut.

Teresita said she and Maurits could come on the last weekend of January, and Ben talked Betty into letting me stay at their house on Saturday night. "She was reluctant at first," he said, "saying the house was too dusty for a guest, but I told her you wouldn't mind. You were an experienced camper."

I was due to leave early Saturday morning and return by Sunday evening, but Teresita called on Friday saying they would be delayed. They couldn't get to me until Saturday afternoon. I called my teenaged babysitter and asked her to watch the kids from 8 AM until 2. I kissed my children goodbye, hoping that Maurits and Tere would show up before the babysitter had to go home.

I called Ben just before leaving, to confirm everything, and he immediately said, "Oh, you're calling to say you can't come because of the forecast. I wouldn't want you to travel alone through the blizzard that's coming."

When I could get a word in, I assured him I was not calling to cancel but to confirm. I didn't think the blizzard would happen anyway. Ben asked me what kind of car I was driving, and when I told him I had a VW Beetle, he sounded greatly reassured.

"Oh, a Beetle can get through anything," he remarked. This was the first I had heard of the magical snowplowing power of Beetles, but I was grateful I wasn't going to have to argue with him about it.

I drove four hours through gray skies and slushy snow to Derry, New Hampshire, listening to the radio and singing along at the top of my lungs with James Taylor:

> Winter, spring, summer, or fall
> All you have to do is call
> And I'll be there, ye, ye, ye
> You've got a friend

I reached Ben's house around noon and picked up Betty for the ride to the hospital. Her face pale and strained, she looked smaller and older than when I had last seen her. She met me on the front step, making me wonder whether she would ever let me into the house.

Ben had written me about Betty's on-going struggles. "I believe Betty is starting to turn the corner now as she is starting to read a little bit every now and then. Her deafness and refusal to have her hearing aid refitted is, I fear, a psychological excuse to hide away in her own almost empty world. My first marriage was wrecked by my poor health. This one is not wrecked—and never will be—but is temporarily stalemated by Betty's health. She is now down to 92 pounds. I am powerless to stop it and have long since decided to leave the matter to time and God."

Betty carried a few things Ben had requested, like his thick wool CPO shirt, and we started off to the hospital. We didn't talk much on the way, just my quiet questions about Ben's health, and her sad replies of "I don't know."

When we entered the hospital, I told Betty to go ahead, as I was going to the bathroom. I wanted her to have a chance to greet her husband without me, and also, after the long drive, I had to go. A few minutes later, as I crossed the lobby to go to Ben's room, I saw Ben and Betty, side by side, waiting for me near the elevators. They looked small, and had a matching air of tentativeness. But perhaps that was my imagination.

I grinned at Ben and shook his hand, and he led us to his single room. A wooden chair stood on each side of the bed. He must have set them up in anticipation of our arrival. He got back onto the bed, fully dressed and on top of the covers, and Betty and I sat on either side of him.

I wish I had held his hand. I wanted to stroke the back of it with my thumb. I was aware that Betty might not like it, though, and that she might have seen it as a competition between us.

We settled in and talked about Ben's prognosis, his level of comfort. He pulled his shirt collar away from his neck and showed us the gauze bandage covering the incision. He was now going to start radiation.

Ben and I talked of the past and the present. Of the rowboat we mended together twenty years before. My pregnancy, and my efforts to sell our house so the boys and I could join Paul in Arizona. Ben and I did all the talking, while Betty listened. I probably talked too much, but I was afraid that, if I stopped, the silence would become a grief that would swallow me entirely. By 4 o'clock, Ben was tiring, so Betty and I left him to have a nap, promising to return in the morning.

I led a silent Betty out of the hospital and through the snow back to the car. I asked what errands she would like to do, since she had me available to drive her anywhere. She asked to go to the grocery store to stock up for Ben's return home in a few days. Once there, Betty went straight to the frozen food aisle and filled the cart with Swanson's TV dinners. I looked with dismay at the growing stack of boxes, and slipped a cooked ham and some fresh vegetables into the cart. I had no faith in Mr. Swanson's integrity or the nutrition in his dinners.

I don't remember unpacking the groceries or eating dinner. I just remember that Betty and I phoned Ben to say goodnight, then went to bed early. It was easier than trying to make more conversation. I slept on a day bed in Ben's study, but before lying down, I poked around his room, looking at the framed newspaper clippings of his Harvard hockey career and the photos of his grown sons.

In the morning, Betty and I ate toaster waffles and got an early start back to the hospital. I would have to leave around noon to get home to my kids in time for Maurits and Tere to return to New York that night.

I fell behind Betty to let her enter Ben's room first. I heard him yelp, "You're early! I haven't even got my trousers buttoned yet." I waited in the hall.

Betty and I again sat in the wooden chairs flanking Ben's bed. He propped two pillows behind his back and sat on top of the covers. He was wearing the CPO shirt Betty had brought him yesterday, and he looked too handsome to be sick.

We talked about the radiation scheduled for him in the following months and about Bas and Peter, waiting at home for me in Connecticut.

If I hadn't missed the boys so fiercely, it would have been hard to leave Ben that day. I would have liked to have stayed until he was discharged from the hospital, then driven him home myself rather than have him drive. I promised him that although I was moving to Arizona, I would return to Cape Cod in July to spend the month with my parents, and I would drive to New Hampshire to see him then.

"We'll see each other again this summer," I smiled.

"We'll build a row boat together," Ben agreed, grinning, "one that floats this time."

Noon arrived and we all stood to say goodbye. When Betty reached up to hug him, he flinched, saying, "Careful of my shoulder." When my turn came, I avoided his wound by putting my left arm on his right shoulder and my right arm around his waist, pulling him close.

"Remember three things," I said softly, "to take good care of yourself, that I love you, and to write to me often."

"Yes," he said, not letting me go. I memorized his warm soapy smell and the feel of his arms around me.

The next month, in February, our house sold, and I moved with the boys to Phoenix. Ben and I continued to write. I told him about Phoenix and the house we were buying. I wrote that I was losing the child I was carrying. He reminded me, during my long month of miscarrying, "Mother Nature is very wise." He wrote of his struggles with radiation. Betty still couldn't get a license and, sick as he felt, Ben drove himself forty miles each way to the hospital for the radiation treatments.

He told me of the visits of his three sons and his first wife, who, one by one, made the trip to Derry to say goodbye to him. He theorized that my next child would be a precocious little girl. He signed his letters to me "Love, Ben."

The last letter I received from Ben was dated March 17. He had never written me as often as I had written him, but by the end of April, when I returned from my father's funeral in Lake Forest, I was so

103

worried by his silence that I called his home. Betty answered.

"Hi, Betty, I'm just calling to see how you and Ben are doing."

"Oh, Laura, Ben died on April 11th."

The silence swallowed me.

Loss

April 1977 was a bad month. My father died, Ben died, and I miscarried.

The Connecticut house had sold in February, and Bas, Peter, and I had moved to Phoenix. where Paul had been on his own starting his job at Ryley, Carlock, and Ralston and studying for the Arizona bar exam.

Paul had been born in Phoenix in 1945, of a Dutch father and American mother. When he was two, they had all moved back to Holland. Now Paul was returning with his own family, to a city full of his kind and generous cousins.

After two months apart, we were overjoyed to be together again, living in the apartment Paul had found, and looking for a permanent house.

I was three months pregnant when I arrived in Phoenix, happy with the sunshine and the smell of orange blossoms, pleased that our family was growing.

The movers arrived and unloaded all our belongings from a large three-bedroom house into the small two-bedroom apartment. We had enough space to put our mattresses on the floor, and to set up the card table and folding chairs, but every other bit of room was stacked with extra furniture. Like hoarders, we wended our way through narrow paths between towering piles of bedframes and sofas.

One Saturday morning, Bas, five, and Peter, two, were eating breakfast with Paul at the card table. Paul knew that I was bleeding, and that it had gotten worse during the night. He looked at me with sadness.

"Can you watch the boys for a while?" I asked. "I'm going to take a bath."

"Sure, we'll walk down to the Circle-K. And maybe," he said, looking solemnly at Bas and Peter, "we'll buy a comic book."

This was met with shouts of approval and a rush of small feet toward the door.

I ran the tub. When I heard the front door close, I got in and lay back in the hot water. My third baby was floating in water inside me, and together we were floating in the water of the tub. But this baby was dying. My tears mixed with bath water and blood.

*   *   *   *

When the bleeding had started, I asked Paul's cousins for a good obstetrician. I made the appointment and showed up for the consultation. The waiting room was cold and unfriendly. The doctor was an austere man who never smiled at me, and as I didn't know him, I couldn't read his expressions. When I told him about the bleeding, he pursed his lips, refused to meet my eyes, and told me to step into the next bleak room for an ultrasound.

The technician was a cheerful young woman. She spread the jelly on my stomach and moved the sensor back and forth over it. When the doctor left to get a phone call, she turned the screen so I could see the prawn-sized baby. When the doctor returned, he told me to make an appointment in one month to have a second ultrasound for comparison, to tell whether the child in me was growing and living, or shrinking and decomposing.

Paul's cousin Sandy invited me to bring the boys and spend each day of that interminable month at her house. I was grateful, because although I didn't know whether it was possible for the bleeding to turn into an enormous hemorrhage and subsequent collapse, I kept imagining the worst. I didn't want the boys to be responsible for me. But still, I taught Bas how to dial 911.

Each day, we showed up at Sandy's house, where my children could play with hers, and she and I, and sometimes other cousins, sat at the kitchen table, drinking cups of coffee, talking about our lives, and solving all the problems of the world. It was like a daycare that accepted mothers.

*   *   *   *

Today in the bathtub I wept, whispering, "I'm sorry," to the baby, searching for why I felt so guilty. "I'm supposed to protect you, and I failed. I didn't create a safe place for you."

I couldn't stay in the bathroom forever. I stood up and ran the shower, washing my hair so I could say I'd gotten soap in my eyes if the boys asked why they were red.

By late March, the month had passed, we had moved into the house on Montebello Avenue, and my parents came to stay for a few days. Taking advantage of the built-in babysitting, I went back to the doctor, and this time when the same technician took the ultrasound, she wasn't bright and cheerful, and she wouldn't swivel the screen toward me. When I asked to see the image, she said that the screen didn't turn. She wasn't a good liar, but I didn't call her on it. I knew what she was seeing.

The doctor came in, looked briefly, and said, "It's smaller. We must schedule you for a D and C."

"I don't want to sound ruthless," I replied, "but my parents are here for the next few days, and if we do this immediately they could look after my boys."

"You don't sound ruthless," he said. "I'll send you home with pre-D and C medication, and we'll do the procedure tomorrow."

The next morning, Paul and I left the boys with my parents, and set off for the Surgicenter. We didn't talk much, but I said, "The doctor told me to wait a month before trying to get pregnant again."

"That's good," he replied. About waiting a month or about getting pregnant again, I wasn't sure. He took his hand off the steering wheel and reached out to hold mine.

When I returned home, Bas and Peter were delighted to see me, even though I'd only been gone a few hours. Paul gave me a kiss and went to work. My mother told me to get into bed and she'd watch the boys. My father brought me a cup of tea. I felt loved and empty at the same time.

Ten months later, our daughter Gabriel was born. There are two and a half years between Bas and Peter, and three and a half between Peter and Gabriel. That empty space is the grave marker for the child of my third pregnancy.

My father and Ben had funerals, and headstones that I could visit to honor them. I don't know of any customs that help you over the grief of a miscarriage. You have to invent your own. There is no funeral, or grave marker, and neighbors don't bring food.

The loss of that child is why I gave blood to the Red Cross each year, because during each pre-donation interview, instead of asking me how many children I've had, they asked how many pregnancies.

The grief eased a little each time I could look the interviewer in the eye and say, "Four."

In Search of Self

In 1982, I entered the master's program in Counseling Psychology at Arizona State University. The kids were growing up, and I wanted to become a therapist. Part of a counseling program explores self-knowledge. Students scrutinize their own interests, activities, moods, and fleeting thoughts in order to learn about themselves. This is done partly, I think, to follow the maxim "to know others you must know yourself," but mostly because we didn't have a handy bunch of other people to examine.

I probably know Paul, my husband of forty-nine years, better than I know myself. My self-study is complicated by my tendency to give myself the benefit of the doubt that some of my more dubious actions are perfectly understandable, while alternately squirming with shame over some of my words or actions that weren't particularly memorable to anyone else. And then there's my difficulty in distinguishing the one type of situation from the other.

The study of the self has a lot in common with the bird watching activities of an ardent ornithologist. I imagine that each of us is given a small mental "Self-Notebook" at our birth, where we can enter our observations about ourselves, trying desperately to identify the whole of what we are seeing from isolated glimpses. The ornithologist, sighting a brief flash of bright red against the green of the rainforest canopy, gives himself credit for the sighting of a Scarlet Macaw. I notice, when I give the last cookie to my small grandchild, that I give myself credit in my Self-Notebook: "generous tendencies, strong family feeling." But it is quite possible that the flash of scarlet was a common Scarlet Tanager, not a Macaw at all, and that I gave away the cookie because I wasn't hungry.

My classmates and I pursued multiple avenues of self-discovery. We were told to keep intimate journals, reviewed only by our professor and his live-in girlfriend, both of whom responded to our deepest thoughts with brief margin notations. We took a great many pencil and paper tests, and we participated in class activities to explore our personalities. One such activity involved us going to opposite sides of the room depending on our answers to the professor's questions.

"Do you belong to a club? Stand against the right wall. If you don't, go to the left wall."

"Do you belong to a sports team? A church group? Do you do volunteer work? Take classes in your hobbies? Entertain friends at your house at least once a month? Go stand against the right wall."

There was a good bit of uncertainty, and students asked questions like, "Does it count if you go to church, but you don't believe in God?" But when all the questions had been asked, and I, like everyone else, had sorted myself out against one wall or the other, we looked enquiringly at the professor to see what he could now tell us about ourselves.

"You against the right wall are Extroverts," he intoned, "and you against the left wall are Introverts."

Bless his heart, I thought, leaning my extroverted self against the introverted wall, the man's as mad as a hatter.

We were given a battery of tests: Strong-Campbell for our career aptitudes, Myers-Briggs for our personality indicators, Minnesota Multiphasic Personality Inventory for our general mental health. We answered questions such as "Would you rather go to a movie with friends, or stay home and organize your sock drawer?" and "Are you afraid of doorknobs? Always or only occasionally?"

We were introduced to the Johari Window as a construct for the personality, and encouraged to fill it out on ourselves. The Johari Window is a square divided into four panes labeled "Open," "Blind," "Secret," and "Unknown."

"Open" is what is easily observable about me and on the surface: I am white, female, and old.

"Blind" is what others see about me, but I don't see about myself. We were given a homework assignment to bring some of our blind spots to our attention.

"Secret" is exactly what it suggests, those things I don't share with others.

"Unknown" is also the unknowable. It represents the part of myself that I hope will be courageous and generous in a crisis, but really I have no idea. Imagine that I am in an overloaded lifeboat in a rough sea. One more survivor swims to my tiny craft and desperately tries to crawl in, threatening to overturn the lot of us into the wintry north Atlantic. Would I help him in? Would I get out and let him have my place instead? Or would I hit him repeatedly over the head with an oar until he went away?

I knew for sure that Paul would find a way to get him into the boat.

The homework for the "Blind" pane consisted of asking friends to tell me my most salient characteristic.

While sitting on the grass in the front yard, drinking a glass of wine with my next door neighbor, as a restorative from our day of chasing small children, I explained the school assignment and asked her to share the first adjective about me that popped into her head.

She paused, and said with an air of weary fortitude, "Really? I haven't ever given you any thought."

I sipped at my wine undaunted, not letting her off the hook.

"Well," she continued, "what jumps into my mind is that you are the least domestic person I have ever met."

My eyes widened, and my pupils probably dilated. I was stunned by the flash of scarlet. Hiding my confusion in my wine glass, I thought, then why have I spent the last ten years of my life at home wiping noses and ironing shirts?

During a lunch break at work, I asked a colleague the same question and got the same discouraging response: "I haven't really thought about you." Chewing his sandwich, he added, "Well, I think you are extremely competitive."

Me? But I'm the person who always lets someone else win at games if they seem to want it badly. Ah, I thought, but I do have to know I could have won, don't I.

I slipped the same question to Garv, my boss at Tumbleweed. He had just stuck his head in my office to ask whether I had fire extinguishers and smoke alarms in my house. "Yes, Garv," I replied, and he nodded as though owning fire extinguishers confirmed everything he'd always felt about me.

Now it was my turn. "What is the first adjective that pops into your head to describe me?"

Garv couldn't pretend he'd never given me any thought. He stopped on his way out the door of my office, and turning back, said, "Well, all I know is that you would nurture anything that couldn't move out of your way in time."

Just like the responses from my neighbor and friend, Garv's response surprised me. Not that I disagreed, necessarily. I was just surprised that he knew it.

I would like to be able to say that I learned a lot about myself after all these academic efforts. But I'd be lying. Pencil-and-paper test results are obscure, and although my neighbor, friend, and boss were probably right in their quick assessments of me, their responses tell me as little about my entire self as the curl of hair in a locket tells about the looks and personality of its original owner.

I did get one step closer to knowing myself in a small flash of illumination a decade or two ago. I was walking alone down a gentle hill in a small town in rural Pennsylvania. I had been sent from Phoenix to do a two-day training with a team of local therapists, and although I had traveled like this before, I hadn't met this team, and was feeling some stage fright. It was a soft rainy autumn morning, and as there were no sidewalks, I was walking along the edge of the street from the parking lot toward the agency's training center, my briefcase in one hand and car keys in the other. As I looked at the sodden leaves in the gutter, I saw a storm drain directly ahead of me.

What if I dropped the keys down the drain? I thought. In my mind's eye I could see them fall, and hear the distant "plonk" as they hit the water far below.

In my imagination, I could see the sympathetic reaction of the waiting therapists when I rushed in the room, breathless with my crisis. I foresaw that they would sit me down and get me coffee and exclaim over my bad luck. We would call the rental car company and then, if that didn't work, we'd call AAA. I would be the center of attention.

On the other hand, my imagination also told me what those therapists would be thinking as they mouthed their soothing words: well, that's the most incompetent woman I've ever met. She can't walk from her car to the office without letting her keys go down the only storm drain in a five-mile radius. She's an Attention Addict, a Crisis Hog, a Moron.

Tempted as I was for that instant to be mothered and coddled, it was too high a price to pay: to trade my appearance of competence for momentary support.

I held on fiercely to my keys, and hurried on.

Having resisted that temptation, I saw once again the flash of the Macaw, and gave myself credit in my Self-Notebook for not having one of the major Personality Disorders: Narcissistic, Histrionic, or Borderline. Although having even considered dropping my keys, I cannot rule out Conduct Disordered.

The labels my friends had given me rang true, and filled in quite a bit of my blind spot. I'm not domestic. I'm competitive, obsessively nurturing, and delinquent.

Part V

Work

The Silver Spoon: You Must Have Delusions of Grandeur to Be Paranoid

I was born with a silver spoon in my mouth. I had kind parents who had plenty of money and created a stable home. Raised in Lake Forest, a rich suburb of Chicago, I was given an elitist education. I feared that if I didn't hide my silver spoon, others would take me for a dilettante: a shallow dabbler in the real world ... someone who is always "slumming."

I was ashamed of that silver spoon. As a child, when new children asked me about my accent—the rather "la-di-da" pronunciation drummed into me by my east coast mother—which I found impossible to shake—I would lie. "My mother is English," I'd say, or "We just moved here from Brazil," wildly naming any place, distant from the Midwest, where it might be assumed that everyone talked as I did.

My discomfort over the advantages I'd been given extended to my education. I grew wary when people found I'd gone to an eastern boarding school or to Stanford.

I spent a lot of time hiding myself.

I might have gone on believing that I was different: simultaneously more than, and less than, everyone else, if it weren't for my boss, Michael Garvey. I went to work for "Garv" as soon as I had accomplished enough of my master's degree to be marketable. I saw a creased "Help Wanted" card on the bulletin board at ASU, advertising an opening for a Youth Care Worker at Tumbleweed, a grass roots agency that assisted runaway, homeless, and delinquent youth.

With a certain degree of anxiety, I went to my job interview, worrying that since overcoming adversity builds character, I, who hadn't had any adversity to speak of, hadn't developed any character. What if the interviewer asked me why I believed I was a suitable candidate to work with delinquent boys? How could my life of ease and privilege qualify me as a Youth Care Worker, or even as a human being? I met with the Program Manager, and happily for me, she didn't ask those questions, so I got the job.

I didn't meet Garv, the Executive Director, until a few weeks later.

Garv was a humorous, bold-tongued, profane, and irreverent Irish

American. He saw courtesy as a false truce, meant to give the insecure a breathing space to rearm themselves with further layers of secrets or self-delusion. He used humor and curiosity about others as a sword to puncture that bubble of bland conformity that each of us depends upon to keep our insecurities out of sight, and our dialogue civilized. He wasn't cruel: his words stung, but they didn't maim. In his own youth, he had been kicked out of every high school in the city of Phoenix, so he had a special place in his heart for delinquents. He had made Tumbleweed a place that respected youth.

Everyone at Tumbleweed seemed to be on a mission to improve me: a self-conscious, well-intentioned, and largely incompetent young woman. It wasn't enough to do your job there. You also had to be comfortable in your own skin as you did it. Delinquent youth are offended by anyone pretending to a self-confidence they don't have. They test each adult's honesty, and forcibly point out where it is lacking.

Hanging out with the Tumbleweed kids gave me a second chance to absorb that lesson of adolescence.

As I left work one day, a boy asked me, "What's that red spot on your nose?" He sat on the front steps of the long, narrow house on 5th Street that was both group home and administrative offices.

"Is that a pimple? Can I pick it?"

I walked around him. "No, Greg," I answered with hauteur. "If I'd wanted it picked, I would have picked it myself."

Like a shark recognizing that his prey is inedible, Greg turned away—for now.

Garv, having more experience and sophistication, could carry my education further.

"What are you wearing?" he asked me one rainy morning.

I had arrived in a waxed yellow sou'wester coat with matching hat and boots. I looked like a garden gnome.

He may never have seen such clothes before. Phoenix doesn't sell a lot of rain gear created for a squall in the north Atlantic.

"Rain gear," I replied cautiously.

"Well, it certainly makes a fashion statement."

"What statement is it making?" I asked, in curiosity as well as trepidation.

"It's saying, 'Fuck it,'" he replied seriously.

I looked down at myself, and had to agree.

In the following years, when I had worked my way up to Program Manager, my office in the Boys' Group Home was only a few feet away from Garv's. By this time, possibly because he had an unerring ability to sense discomfort, just as the boys could, I had become an object of fascination to him. He would periodically stick his head in my door with peremptory questions. The first time he did this, it took me completely by surprise.

"Did you go to Stanford?"

I felt a sudden clench of alarm. "Yes, Garv," I replied, continuing to erase the mistakes I had made on the staff work schedule.

Garv nodded to himself as though fitting a piece into a jigsaw puzzle, and without comment walked back to his own office.

Another day, I sat at my desk half working on the budget, and half looking out my office window at the man on the corner of Roosevelt and 5th Street who was slowly sinking to the pavement. Was he having a drug overdose or a heart attack?

Garv stuck his head in my door and demanded, "Were you a debutante?"

"Yes, Garv," I replied, my face reddening, and I turned toward the phone to dial 911 for the crumpling stranger.

A month later, Garv pounced into my office, startled by a new thought. "Did your parents send you away to boarding school?"

"Yes, Garv," I replied, listening with one ear to the shouted greetings of ten adolescent males, home from the library, and the scolding voice of the Youth Care Worker to one unfortunate boy. "I don't care if you did run out of time for your research project and wanted to finish it at home!" she yelled. "If you ever rip pages out of the *Encyclopedia Britannica* again, I will personally make you copy the entire set!"

Garv turned to greet the boys streaming past him and then walked back to his office without saying more. He never asked me what it was like to go to boarding school, or to Stanford, or to be a debutante. He seemed satisfied simply that his suspicions had been confirmed. In doing so, he skewered each of my secret sensitivities.

Each time I answered Garv in the affirmative and he returned to his office to mull over what he'd learned, I was left to wonder why he had asked it. My insecurities suggested that he was pigeonholing me as an elitist, and building a case in his head that I was too shallow to work with real people who had real problems.

One hot summer afternoon, while I was trying to think of a new way to ask the City of Phoenix for grant money, Garv stuck his head in my office and asked in an entirely different tone of voice, "Do you think your parents loved you?"

"Yes, Garv," I answered softly, looking up at him and waiting for more.

But he just left, looking puzzled.

So was I.

For reasons of his own that I never understood, Garv opened me up and rummaged around inside me, shining the searchlight of his attention on every area of my life that represented unearned privilege. With the force of a battering ram and the accuracy of a stiletto, he nosed out every unfair advantage that I had been given. He toughened me up and set me on my feet. I owe him a tremendous debt.

Tumbleweed Kids

Not every boy or girl who passed through Tumbleweed's group homes survived. We could keep them alive as long as they were with us, but we couldn't prevent them from running away and ending up dead.

Thessalyn was beautiful and fierce. I opened the door for her when she arrived at Tumbleweed. She strode in just ahead of her parole officer. She was a tall girl, with bright black eyes and honey brown skin. Her head was high and her hands were cuffed behind her back. She sat on the group home sofa, her arms twisted uncomfortably, unable to lean back.

"Take the handcuffs off her," I said to the P.O. "She's in a halfway house now."

"Well, you may be sorry," he replied, slowly unlocking the cuffs.

Thessalyn ran away from us within days. Two weeks later, her parole officer called to tell us she had been found dead of an overdose in the bathroom of a Tucson nightclub.

*   *   *   *

One winter afternoon, I was raking leaves with Tyrone and other boys in the backyard of their group home. Tyrone was always serious. I never saw him laugh. Handsome and dark, he showed a flash of white teeth when he squinted against the sun. The boys turned to him with questions of how to do the job, and he divided the tasks fairly, working hard at it himself. The boys followed his lead without question.

Tyrone and I raked our way to the same corner of the yard at one point. We leaned on the low wall for a moment to admire the progress. Neat piles of leaves were being shoveled into bags by the other boys.

"You might consider going into the Army," I said. "If you were my squad leader I'd have confidence that you could keep me alive."

"Mmph," said Tyrone, with a twist of his lips. He opened his mouth as though he were about to say more, but suddenly turned away and returned to raking.

Tyrone ran away from us.

I heard later that he died in a suicide-by-cop. He stole a car. When police surrounded him, he hid behind the car and drew a gun. The police drew theirs and shouted at him not to be a fool and to drop his.

"Oh, I wouldn't hurt you," he said, standing.

They shot him.

Tyrone's family dropped his things off with us after his death. Perhaps because they didn't want them, and we were his last address. They left everything their son had owned in one green, plastic garbage bag.

Not every youth AWOLed. Most finished their time with Tumbleweed and returned to their families.

*   *   *   *

I met David when he first came to Tumbleweed at fourteen—a handsome, sturdy boy, his hair kept short to hide the curls. He had the soft, almost imperceptible accent of people who speak Spanish at home. I have known him now, mostly through phone calls and correspondence, for thirty years.

Like Tyrone, David was another of the fierce, proud youth who make natural leaders. He was chosen by the Department of Juvenile Corrections to be a member of a youth panel to talk to parole officers, policemen, and judges about the problems kids face that get them into trouble with the law, and what society could do about it. I was his chaperone and chauffeur to the conference.

David wasn't impressed by the honor of speaking at the annual Juvenile Corrections conference, but I was. When we arrived, he was given a blue ribbon to wear around his neck, with his name badge hanging from it. He sat on a panel with other youth and answered the audience's questions with a calm confidence. David did everything confidently.

David spoke of his rough neighborhood, and the necessity of fighting the older boys who disrespected his sister on the way home from school.

A police officer in the audience asked, "Couldn't you have ignored them and kept walking?"

"If I did that, the disrespect would have gotten worse the next day."

"Couldn't you have told your teachers, or your parents?" another asked.

"If I'd snitched, they'd have killed me. I had to take care of it myself."

The audience was stymied. I watched David, proud of him. Once

120

again he was standing up to the more powerful. He wasn't backing down. He wasn't fighting, and he wasn't running away. Maybe he'd make it in the world this time.

But I was wrong. By the time he was twenty-four, David had been tried and sentenced to twenty-one and a half years in prison.

I don't know what crime David committed. I have never asked him outright, although I've given him opportunities to tell me. Giving him privacy is my way of giving him respect. It is not my business. David is paying the price for his crime.

David calls me about once a month, and writes me twice a month. I send him money for stamps and phone calls. He has been navigating the difficult world of prison for twenty years now. He used to get in trouble, but hasn't done so in years. On a recent phone call, I asked him how he had made that change.

"Well," he said, his voice echoing on the phone line, "when I first came to prison I was angry. I was young and I had so long to serve that I couldn't see the light at the end of the tunnel. I fought and disrespected, and it was a relief. It wouldn't make any difference anyway. I spent my first year and two months in lockdown, in a cell twenty-three hours a day."

I tried to imagine what that solitude had been like, and what it must have done to him.

"But my mom would come a long way to visit me, and the visits were just thirty minutes. There was a glass window between us. The lockdown visitation room had a vending machine for the visitors and families, and I told my mom to get herself a soda to drink, but she said, 'If you can't have one, then I don't want one.' It broke my heart."

Choices, I thought. She took the choice he would remember.

"I wanted to see my mom smile," David continued. "I wanted to hug her and hold her hand, so I made some changes that would be better for me and that would ease her pain."

"So you made the decision not to get in trouble," I said, "but how do you do that day after day?"

"Well," he said, "you stick to your own. The mess hall is divided and you sit with your race. But even so, you still have groups in each race, made of the strong or the weak. No matter where you are, you will always have those who prey upon the weak."

"What if you see that happening in front of you. What do you do?"

"If you see trouble coming, sometimes you can turn around or step into the library, and not be there when it happens."

"And if you don't see it coming?"

"Yeah. Then, if it doesn't have to do with you, you keep on moving, but if it does involve you or your race, you act on your decision. You have to make your choice at that moment."

The robotic operator came on the line telling us we had one more minute.

"I gotta go, Laura. I'll write you more about it in a letter. Take care."

"Take care, David."

As far as I can tell, the world that David lives in hasn't changed much from his old neighborhood when he was a boy. Unlike my world, his is often violent, and the stakes for a misstep very high.

David will get out of prison in one year and three months. He will face the same challenges to his honor and his courage. Will he have more choices this time? Will he be able to distinguish courage from violence, and cooperation from weakness?

I can't imagine myself succeeding at what society is asking him to do—start again in a world he hasn't seen in over two decades. But then, I can't figure out what he could have done differently as a child, when he had to stop the bullies preying upon his sister. Both for her sake and his own.

Predators and Prey

Winter evenings in the desert get dark by 6 o'clock. As I led my group of five adolescent males across the prison yard to the library, a solitary owl, with a wingspan as broad as the reach of my arms, angled its body to swoop between us. Its speed and silence scared the conversation right out of us.

Summer evenings after a monsoon rain are filled with the mutterings of toads. The ground was covered with them. The boys and I had to watch our step. They blew themselves up as big as footballs to scare us away. The boys left my side to dropkick them over the fence. I hurried everyone along as fast as I could.

For ten years, I worked as a counselor under contract to the Department of Juvenile Corrections. For most of those years, my substance abuse groups and individual mental health sessions were held at Black Canyon School, a juvenile prison, out in the middle of the desert.

Although my main job was at Tumbleweed—forty hours a week for twenty-eight years, I always had a variety of second and third jobs that lasted about ten years apiece: instructor of psychology at Phoenix College, clinical consultant for the counseling model Functional Family Therapy, and chairman of the Board of Behavioral Health. At this time, 1987-95, my second job was with the Department of Juvenile Corrections.

Two evenings a week, I drove up Route 17, past the *Do Not Pick Up Hitchhikers* signs, and took the Happy Valley exit into the desert, following the narrow macadam road that led to Black Canyon School. At that time, Black Canyon and Adobe Mountain, two contiguous juvenile prisons just north of Phoenix, euphemistically called schools, had slightly different populations. Adobe Mountain School held the general juvenile male offenders, and Black Canyon School held the mental health juvenile male offenders.

Both prisons were surrounded by a high chain link fence topped with triple rolls of razor wire. A section of the chain link and razor wire also separated the two prisons and the two sets of boys.

Unlike my job of counseling delinquent youth at Tumbleweed, where I was usually greeted with a groan and the comment "Oh, it's you again," counseling at the prison was very good for my morale. I would enter the prison gates, sign in, and walk across the yard of grass, sand, and pebbles to be greeted at the dormitory with cries of "Laura, Laura, can I see you this evening? I need to talk to you."

Some of those voices didn't even belong to my clients, just kids joining in the general din of excitement. The boys could either talk to me in the library or sit in their cells. It wasn't my choice or theirs who came. Like every other aspect of their lives, access to counseling was decided by the prison officials.

Each evening between 5:00 and 9:00, I held one hour-long group session for five boys, and then three individual sessions. Since no documents could leave the prison, at the end of each evening I sat at one of the tables in the small library room to write up my case notes. It helped to do it immediately so that the boys' stories wouldn't run together in my mind. If I had been allowed to wait until I got home, I might have forgotten whether it was Kyle's mother who shot herself and Shane's mother who hung herself, or the other way around.

The counseling groups were supposed to be about the prevention and reduction of substance abuse, but since the boys had not used drugs since getting locked up, they unanimously thought they no longer had a problem. No counselor wants to be the voice of doom in the face, however unrealistic, of client hope. I didn't want to look at them gloomily and say, "Oh, yes, you do indeed have a problem, and unless you attend my groups you are screwed."

Instead, I asked them where they would be if they weren't locked up, and most gave the same response: "I'd be dead by now."

So we worked on the skills that would keep them alive: stopping to think before you act, how to make decisions, how to recognize options and make a plan, how to talk to others, how to solve problems or negotiate solutions without running away or numbing yourself.

As they talked, the boys made a hundred comments that broke my heart, while I sat there listening with a calm I didn't feel.

Jeremy, looking in the bag of candy I'd brought each boy for Hallowe'en, said, "Oh, a Pixie Stick. My stepfather always gave me one of those to stop me crying after he molested me."

When Jeremy had turned fourteen, he felt he was old enough to run away from his home and his stepfather. He stole a car that he didn't know how to drive, and took it north on the highway. Rounding a bend, he lost control and crossed into oncoming traffic. The accident killed a pregnant woman.

Without a decent adult in their lives, the boys became both

predators and prey.

After group was finished and I'd returned my five boys to the guards at their dorm, I would call for my first individual client.

"Where's Jake?" I asked the most approachable female guard when I couldn't find him.

"He was belligerent this afternoon, picking fights with everyone. He's been sent to solitary and can't come to your session." Her eyes held a gleam of satisfaction in telling me this, more I thought in opposition to me than to Jake.

"Can I go to him?"

"I suppose so," she replied without expression, "but they won't let you in, or him out."

If ever a kid could use a counseling session, I thought, it was when he was in solitary.

On my way across the yard, I saw three guards talking together in a pool of light. I stopped to ask them whether I could take Jake to counseling or get him out early.

They gave me an immediate and unanimous "No." They talked to me about rules, and the importance of them.

I found Jake by standing on tiptoe, peering through each high, small window in the row of solitary cells. I could see him, a pale, drooping boy in a barren room, sitting on the concrete frame of a bed molded to the floor. Even his limp blond hair had given up. I tapped the glass.

He looked up from his hands to see my head from the eyes up. He came over to the door and touched the thick glass. The only way we could hear each other was to shout.

Looking down, I saw a two-inch gap where the door didn't quite meet the threshold, perhaps for air or ease of mopping. I motioned Jake to sit down on the floor near it, and on my side I slid down too.

Now, though we couldn't see each other, we were close enough to the gap to talk.

"Are you OK?" I asked.

"Yeah, I wasn't earlier, but I'm OK now. Can you tell them I'm calm, and get me out of here?"

"I've tried, Jake, but they tell me that you've got to take your consequence. They'll let you out in twenty-four hours if you stay calm."

We talked a bit about what had upset him—nothing and everything. He'd had no mail and no visits, and another boy, noticing his disappointment at mail call, had laughed and said, "Your mother's probably too busy fucking one of her boyfriends to write you."

Jake punched him, and everyone else he could reach.

Slowly, Jake and I ran out of words.

On either side of the door, we sat on the floor back to back. I saw motion out of the corner of my eye, the tips of Jake's fingers extending toward me under the door.

I laced my fingers in his, and we sat in his solitude.

Fire

It's the summer of 1989, and I'm bringing a girl from Tumbleweed's halfway house to bury the man she loved.

The parking lot is nearly empty when I drive up—just an old blue sedan parked in the shade of the single mesquite tree, and off in the far corner, a dusty white bus, with *Maricopa County Jail* in big black letters on its side. Radio music comes from the open windows of the bus. I pull my car just to the left of the sedan to get a bit of shade.

Far to the west of Phoenix, the large dirt graveyard for indigents is bordered on one side by the Jackson and Perkins experimental rose fields, and beyond those, the White Tank Mountains. The other three sides are desert and dust.

The colors of the rose fields echo the mountain range in the distance: pinks and purples that fade into the blue.

Seventeen-year-old Alicia sits next to me in the passenger seat, and her mother—whose name I never catch, or perhaps am never given—sits in the back. Alicia, slender and brown-skinned, had been paroled to Tumbleweed's Girls' House where I am the program manager. She had served her time for drug running. She hates parole, the group home, her mother, and me.

Alicia gets out of the car, slamming her door, and comes face to face with a middle-aged man in a black suit just getting out of the sedan next to us.

"Hello, I'm Reverend Carlson," he says, extending his hand to Alicia.

Alicia looks at the hand but doesn't take it.

Her mother moves past her and takes his hand. The mother and the minister are a contrast: she short and plump, the buttons of her faded blouse gapping across her waist, and he tall and bony, his black suit hanging on him, touching only at his shoulders, his shirt collar limp from the heat.

I motion Alicia ahead to the open grave and the group of eight prisoners in gray and white striped jumpsuits standing around it. As we approach, all but four of the men shoulder their shovels and return to the bus. When they disappear inside it, the radio suddenly stills. The four remaining men, holding broad straps to lower the plywood coffin

127

into the hole, take a respectful step back, shoulder to shoulder on the far side of the grave. They double the number of mourners.

A fierce heat radiates from Alicia, but whether she is going to scream or run or hit or faint, I can't tell. Her mother watches her anxiously, hands clasped in prayer, but fingers never still. She flicks her glance away each time Alicia catches her looking.

*   *   *   *

Every day for the past week, I had driven Alicia to the Maricopa County Burn Unit to visit her boyfriend Michael. Boyfriend is a patronizing word in the context of death. She visited her lover. During each drive from the group home to the hospital and back again, she yelled at me—furious that she hadn't been there with him, angry at parole for separating them, angry at me for enforcing parole. She wanted to have been behind him on his motorcycle when it crashed into the truck, skidding along the pavement to burst into flame.

"I would have had my arms around his waist," she said. "We would have been together."

You'd be dying too, I thought.

"I could have saved him," she said, her teeth clenched and her eyes straight ahead.

I flinched at the anger in her words, and wished I could have told her about grief I'd felt in my life—a companionship of grief—but she might have seen it as competition. Right now she was angry at me only in a general way, because I was handy. I wouldn't give her information about my life to use against me.

I'd been carefully taught that lesson by another grieving Tumbleweed girl the year before. When I had told Claire I was sorry for the loss of her mother, she had railed at me, and cursed my children, wishing them dead, so I could feel the same pain she did.

For a while, I worried that she had power. I checked that my children were safe in their beds every night. Gradually, I thought about her words less often. She made me cautious around other people's grief.

Alicia sat by Michael's bed each day until he died. Her hands moved restlessly, unable to find an unburned place to touch him. This handsome, black-haired boy who'd visited Alicia at Tumbleweed and teased her to make her laugh was now covered by bandages, his impish eyes closed. A few members of his family came to visit. They looked briefly at his still form, said a few words to Alicia, and then went away again.

Alicia murmured constantly to Michael, but he was deep in medically induced unconsciousness. Leaning against the wall by the door, watching her bend over the bed, and him never moving, I grieved for them both.

We stayed in the quiet, dimly lit burn ward for hours each day, until I told her it was time for me to go back to work. She hated me for pulling her away, but she came.

* * * *

Looking around the graveyard, I wonder where Michael's family is. Only Alicia's mother had been willing to come with us.

The minister stands at the head of the grave, holding his Bible against his chest, squinting at the sky.

The prisoners, solid and competent, watch us with kind eyes. They gaze longest at Alicia.

Alicia holds herself tightly, arms across her chest. She doesn't cry.

The minister clears his throat, opens his Bible to the place marked with a dark ribbon. "'I am the Resurrection and the Life,' saith the Lord,'" he begins. I look out over the roses and the mountains, thinking about the boy released from pain, and this girl left behind.

I want to put my arm around Alicia's shoulders, but she would never tolerate my touch. I stand as close as I can, the air between us shimmering with rage.

Getting to Know You

Approaching Derek's trim ranch-style home for the first time, I felt my usual stage fright. What would I find on the other side of this door? Could I be useful to them?

I knocked. When an old man opened the door, I introduced myself as the family counselor sent by Juvenile Corrections. He said he was Derek's step-grandfather.

"I'm the only one here just now. My wife is picking Derek up from school on her way home from work. They should be home any minute."

I smiled and nodded, while he indicated with a sweep of his hand that I should sit in one of the chairs at the dining room table.

I hesitated. I didn't want to take the wrong chair.

Looking at the table, I saw Grandfather's chair must be the one next to the full ashtray with a smoking cigarette balanced on the rim. The one next to his might be Grandmother's. I took the chair across from them.

Grandfather and I chatted about the heat of the summer evening, and the shade provided by the big trees in his neighborhood. After that, he became quiet, seeming to listen for footsteps at the front door. It didn't seem to me that he had run out of things to say, just that he didn't want his family to find him talking to me, for fear they might think he was betraying their secrets. He punctuated the silence with an occasional deep, wet cough that shook his thin body, making it hard for him to catch his breath. Then he lit another cigarette.

The front door opened again, and a tall, dark-haired teenager strode in, followed by an elderly woman who was still finishing her sentence: "...and put your backpack in your room. I don't want it left in the hall again."

This must be Derek, recently released from juvenile prison and ordered to attend family counseling as one of the conditions of his parole, and his grandmother. The records said she had raised him since he was a toddler.

They joined me at the table. I stood up to be able to change chairs if I'd taken the wrong one. My guess hadn't been bad, at least not so bad as to be worthy of comment. Grandmother sat next to

Grandfather, and Derek sat on my side of the table, leaving one chair vacant between us as a safe zone.

Now, introductions over, I had to talk enough so the family knew what I was thinking. It almost didn't matter what I said at this stage, as long as it was easy and positive. I had to sound confident enough to suggest I could be useful to them, without the arrogance to imply that I knew the solution to their problems. That I could have managed their lives better than they had.

I handed the intake paperwork to each one and explained it, searching my purse for pencils and pens. The questionnaires asked hard questions about drug and alcohol use, violence, and suicidal thoughts. Each person, in the privacy of his own relationship with the paper, would get warmed up to the idea that once written down, the answers were no longer secret, and it would be a short step to putting these thoughts into words and saying them in front of each other.

The pencils scratched along the pages. I looked at each bent head, trying to estimate the impact that they would have on my life. Therapy is supposed to change the recipients, but it is a two-way street. We are all changed in some way by intimate contact with one another.

One by one, they raised their heads and returned the pencils. They looked at me expectantly, as they might at a doctor who, having reviewed their X-rays, could tell them what was wrong, and what further painful procedures must be endured to fix it.

But I am not a doctor, and I don't have the answers, just curiosity and optimism carried on the backs of a great many questions.

Derek's grandfather hid behind the smoke of another cigarette and cast an anxious glance sideways to his wife. She gave me a blue-eyed glare, daring me to tell her that her grandson's problems were in any way her fault, or his, either, for that matter. I could see, by the constant activity of her fingers, curling and uncurling a small scrap of paper, that she was controlling her pent-up energy. I imagined that she had all her arguments lined up and was eager to get right down to the task of defending herself from my imagined accusations.

Derek didn't look at any of us. He pushed his chair back from the table and stared at his enormous sneakers, letting his hair fall over his eyes, an attempt to defy us all and disappear. His fists were shoved deep into his pockets, canting his body like the long hypotenuse to the right angle of his chair.

He was listening, though. He seemed to be waiting for his family to reveal all his failures and character flaws to a stranger, and then for me to preach the same sermons that he had heard before from family, teachers, police, judge, and parole officer. He seemed impatient for us to get on with it, so that he could dismiss us and get back to his life.

I knew what I had to do, but not necessarily how to do it. I had to help them relax and see their challenges as puzzles to be solved, not failures to be ashamed of. I wanted to strengthen their relationships with each other, not have them focus only on self-protection.

We wouldn't be done simply when they could talk and listen to each other. We also had to find solutions to some of the problems they faced.

Not the issues that I thought were problems. But the ones they did.

I had to listen, and question, and modify my understanding, question again, and clarify, until I saw the world through their eyes, and understood what they saw as their problems, and possible solutions.

Derek's grandmother said in a matter-of-fact voice that she and his step-grandfather were looking forward to moving to Mexico as soon as Derek turned eighteen in six months. I asked if Derek would go with them, and his grandmother said, "No."

I asked if this was a problem, leaving Derek on his own at eighteen, and they all said, "No," in unison.

Grandmother said she had raised Derek almost all his life. She told me she had adopted his mother when she was an infant, but as a teenager, the mother had developed mental health and addiction problems. "I'm old now," she said, leaning toward me and looking me straight in the eye. "I'm done with all that responsibility. I want to sit on a beach and sip a margarita."

Derek sat up straight. "Leave my mother out of this. You've always been ashamed of her."

"I haven't always been ashamed, but I'm tired of rescuing her. She called me this morning while I was at work, saying she's homeless again. She said her pit bull killed her landlord's shepherd, and he kicked her out."

"But," said Derek, leaning toward his grandmother, "you only meet with her when there's a crisis."

Grandmother spoke softly and directly to Derek. "Yes, I am ashamed of her now, since she got the row of swastikas tattooed on her forehead."

I intervened with small words of common sense. "You have every right to be protective of your mother, Derek. But a mother has a right to criticize her daughter, just as much as a son has a right to defend her. Your grandmother's relationship to your mother is as close as yours."

They looked at each other with some surprise.

Slowly, over the course of many sessions, their concerns emerged. No one, not the family, nor Derek, nor the parole officer, nor I, were worried that Derek would live a life of crime. Although juvenile parole was paying for counseling, crime was not the problem, as they saw it.

As the weekly meetings continued, everyone's focus shifted. I was no longer as aware of my surroundings, and much more aware of the nuances of words and gestures. The family was able to pick right up where they left off the previous week, without worrying about what I would think about what they were saying.

Derek didn't mind his grandparents leaving him when they went to Mexico. He didn't want to go with them. But what did bother him was that he didn't know how to rescue his mother from her self-destruction.

I asked Derek about the tattoo on his forearm, figuring it must be important to him. "Who is Joshua?" I asked.

"That's my younger brother. Who died. I should have saved him," Derek said. "I'd have a brother now."

"You couldn't have saved him," Grandmother intervened. Turning to me, she said, "Derek wasn't quite three years old when his baby brother slipped between the mattress and the crib rails and suffocated. That's when I took Derek to live with me."

"You shouldn't have taken me from my mother. That left her all alone."

"She was an adult."

"Then you should have taken her in when you took me," Derek said, staring at his hands.

"I couldn't. Her drug use was out of control."

I asked if they wanted to invite Derek's mother to join the sessions. They looked at each other in silence, then all turned to me to say, "No."

Step-grandfather had a grandson of his own, named Luke, who had also lived with them once. When Luke was a child, he lived in foster care group homes. His grandfather had visited him occasionally—the only family member to do so—and Luke had loved him ever since. At eighteen, when Luke aged out of foster care, he came to live with his grandfather and step-grandmother. But Luke had mental health issues, and when he turned twenty, and still wouldn't work or go to school, the grandparents had told him to live on his own. Luke was twenty-one now, homeless, and living nearby, in a tent they had given him.

I was beginning to get an idea of what the problems were in this family, although the family members were still too close to them to see a pattern or put it into words. I requested that they locate Luke, and invite him to join our sessions. He showed up the following week.

When we were all at the table again, I said a few words to bring Luke up to date, and to let the family contradict me if my understanding was wrong. "Your family seems to me to have a strong value of responsibility to each other: grandparents to mother, Derek to mother, grandparents to Derek, and grandparents to you, Luke. I think that it's difficult to balance the value of responsibility to others with responsibility to yourself."

Grandfather put down his cigarette and said, "I don't feel a responsibility to protect Luke. I tried to do that when he was younger. But I do feel a responsibility to get him independent. I want Luke to get a job." Grandfather picked up his cigarette and stubbed it out in disgust.

Luke wouldn't look up to meet his grandfather's gaze.

"He might have to move to another town to get work," Grandfather continued. "I'd help him find a new place to live near where he found work. But he won't even consider it. He'd rather stay homeless and live in a tent."

Wouldn't or couldn't consider it? I wondered.

Luke was silent, staring at his hands on the table. He had to listen to his grandfather tell a stranger that he was incapable of self-reliance. Grandmother and Derek stayed quiet, keeping their eyes on the table and their thoughts to themselves.

I looked at Luke's bowed head and said, "I'm guessing that you don't want to move away because you worry about your grandfather's health."

"Yes!" he said, looking up for the first time. "His cough is worse, and I love him."

The family value of responsibility included Luke's relationship to his grandfather.

I told the family about how to find services for homeless young adults over eighteen, case management to help Luke find training, a job, and housing.

Luke said he could never go for an interview on his own.

"I'll go with you if you want," Derek said, "and explain things."

A Thorough Education

At 6:50 AM, I left the teachers' lounge at Phoenix College and walked to my classroom. As I approached the door, my stomach clenched. Instead of entering, I made a sharp left and went to the women's restroom. Every single morning of my first semester teaching Psychology 101, my stomach clenched and I had to detour. Apparently, my stomach could see the approach of the classroom door.

Every day, I thanked my stomach for reacting before class started.

Having gotten myself successfully into the classroom, I spread my papers out on the desk at the front of the room, and placed the half-podium on top of the desk. The blackboard was behind me, with plenty of chalk in the lip. The students began to file in, chattering together in twos and threes. Male, female, old, young, they represented every demographic.

For the first week, I released my nervous energy by letting my fingers play in the chalk dust that had accumulated on the shelf inside the mobile podium. While I stood behind it, talking or listening to my students' questions, my fingers were never still. They danced jigs, wrote unmentionable words and erased them, climbed the interior walls, and did hand pushups. At one point the class started laughing, and I asked what was so funny.

"You realize there is no back to that podium, don't you?" came a voice from the second row. "We can see your fingers."

No, I hadn't realized that. I stopped playing in the chalk dust.

I had been a student at Phoenix College myself for two years, catching up on the undergraduate psychology classes I needed to get into the counseling master's program.

Now, six years later, I'd finished the master's degree and had been working as a counselor at Tumbleweed for several years. I had met a good many delinquent youth, and thought it would be interesting to meet some normal youth: kids who were in college instead of on parole.

There must have been some "normal" youth in my classes. After all, by the time I stopped teaching, I had taught two sections every semester for ten years: 1,600 students. But the students I remember with great affection are the ones who had personal and painful experience with the psychological concepts we studied.

Normal is overrated.

Teaching the content of Psychology 101 was the least of the challenges. Figuring out how to help so many different people learn was harder.

At the same time, I learned a lot from the students. Each one taught me a different lesson. Many had chosen to go back to school to train for a new job after some traumatic incident ended their ability to perform their old one. They had courage and dignity.

*   *   *   *

John, a man in his fifties, had lost his left arm in a car accident and could no longer be a machinist. He was in college to prepare himself for another career. He wore a band around the stump of his arm and could administer a gentle electrical stimulation when the pain got too bad. He knew a lot about the mind-body-emotion-behavior connection from his own life, and could tell the class about it.

*   *   *   *

When we got to the chapter on functional and dysfunctional families, Claire, a Chinese American girl, raised her hand.

"In my culture, only boys are valued," she began. "When my grandparents come to visit, they bring presents for my brother, never for me. He sits in the living room and talks to the adults while I help my mother serve them food and drinks. My family is sending him to college. I must find my own way.

"My family isn't dysfunctional," she said. "It functions fine. It's just wrong." With that, she closed her mouth, lowering her eyes to her desktop.

*   *   *   *

Jacob taught me the lesson of a teacher's impact. A skinny, red-headed boy of nineteen, Jacob raised his hand in response to every point of the lecture, but seldom had anything relevant to say. He appeared to have brain damage. Once he started talking, he was difficult to stop. I was uncomfortable, but I did what I knew to do from social situations. I interrupted him with a "thank you" and asked him to let others respond to his thoughts. I told him we had limited time and had to move on. Nothing worked.

Things got worse. The class began rolling their eyes when he raised his hand. He seemed completely unaware that his behavior was different from theirs. When the other students began to groan audibly, and Jacob looked around to see what they were groaning about, I had to do something different.

I left the podium and walked over to stand in front of Jacob. I listened carefully to what he was saying, and waited for a pause. I said that his idea was a good one. The class looked at me in surprise. I was surprised by their surprise. Had I been teaching them that I was disdainful of Jacob, rather than just inexperienced and out of my depth? Were they groaning in a misguided attempt to align themselves with authority and support me?

After my words of praise, the class stopped reacting against Jacob, and he also calmed down a bit. Perhaps he had always been more aware than I thought.

When we got to the chapter on learning and memory, Jacob raised his hand and said that he had trouble with remembering anything now.

"My stepfather was angry at me one day when I got home," Jacob said, fiddling with his pencil. "He was waiting for me in the driveway. When I got off my bike, he began hitting me with a baseball bat. I tried to cover my head with my arms, but I guess I didn't do it right."

The classroom was silent. All eyes were on Jacob, and Jacob's eyes were on me.

"A neighbor called the police, and they stopped him when they arrived. But it took them a while to come. My brain doesn't work like it used to anymore."

At the end of class, as the students were filing out, one boy called out, "Hey, Jacob, do you have class next hour, or do you want to get a Coke with us at the cafeteria?"

*   *   *   *

Psychology is based on a combination of philosophy and learning theory. The object is to help people understand their past and decide what they want for their future. To do this, sometimes they have to unlearn old beliefs that are not true, and relearn new ones. The tools to create learning are teaching, persuading, and influencing: the tools of learning theory.

Even though I stood at the front of the room lecturing, I wanted the students to doubt me, to question and challenge. Please, I thought, don't stop learning at the limits of what I know. Push on past. Accepting authority is too easy. Sheep probably admire their shepherd, as he leads them gently to slaughter.

On the day we were discussing cause and effect versus correlation, I brought in a current newspaper clipping about urban crime.

"Don't just accept what you read in the paper without question. That the crime rate is high and the neighborhood is largely black and Hispanic is correlation. This article suggests that being a part of a racial minority causes you to commit more crimes. How did they eliminate all the other variables such as poverty, oppression, despair? Prove to me it's a character flaw in a race, not a product of society instead. Stop and think. Question authority. Ask for sources. Think for yourselves."

*   *   *   *

During the one semester when I had a deaf man in the class, I discovered that human interaction is vital to me. There is no substitute for learning face to face.

The department head told me that I would be getting a deaf student, named Charles. He could read lips, and would only get a sign language interpreter if that didn't work. I was very aware of Charles, a handsome boy in his early twenties, neatly dressed in a button down shirt and khaki trousers, sitting in the front row, leaning forward slightly to watch my face. However, much as I wanted him to succeed, I didn't seem able to face him uninterruptedly. Too often I turned to face another student or to write something on the blackboard behind me.

I got a memo from the Psychology Department, informing me that this wasn't working, and that Charles would start bringing a sign language interpreter from now on.

The interpreter was a pleasant, nondescript woman who sat in a chair to the immediate right of where I stood at the podium, and directly in front of Charles. She signed every word I said. She signed if I talked while turning to the board, or walking along the aisles handing back test papers. She signed what the students sitting behind Charles were saying to me.

The class watched her avidly. They listened to my voice and watched her hands.

It is unnerving to talk to a large group and never get eye contact. Sometimes I was so desperate for acknowledgment of my existence that I would lean down farther and farther until the interpreter and I were practically cheek to cheek. Several pairs of eyes would then flick briefly to my face before returning permanently to her hands.

Charles did well in school and went on to Gallaudet University the next year, to complete his bachelor's degree.

*   *   *   *

Another student, Suzanne, arrived at class one lovely spring morning with a large bandage around her hand. We stood in the hallway after class, as she tried to tell me about what was happening to her. Trying to talk with Suzanne was like taking the proverbial drink out of a fire hydrant. Her words came so fast they were nearly incomprehensible. I put my hands on her arms and gently pressed.

Looking in her eyes, I said, "Slow your words, Suzanne. What's going on?"

"NothingreallyIjusthurtmyhandandstoppedtakinglithiumsoIcouldtaketheantibioticsbutnowitsreallyhardsittinginclassordoingthereading."

My hands on her arms had difficulty slowing the rapid motion of her gestures.

She had fallen rollerblading and gone to an urgent care clinic for antibiotics. The doctor had asked what other medicines she was taking. Not wanting to reveal herself to a stranger, Suzanne had said, "None."

She filled her antibiotic prescription and then decided that she should stop taking her Lithium for bipolar disorder, because she didn't know what the drug interaction would be.

"Suzanne. I think you're having a manic episode."

"Youreallythinkso?" Her gaze darted all around me.

"Yes, I really think so. You should go back to your doctor with the lithium and the antibiotic and ask him if you can take them together. Do you have a ride?"

"Yesmyboyfriend'swaitingforme.I'llgonow.Ihadnoidea."

I learned from Suzanne that the greatest difference between my college students and my counseling clients was that the college students occasionally cooperated with me.

*   *   *   *

I was only an adjunct instructor at Phoenix College, with a full-time job at Tumbleweed, but I still had to have office hours on campus. So each day, I got to school an hour before my seven o'clock class. Usually I graded papers or prepared lectures, because for some reason, no student had ever asked to talk to me during office hours. During the winter months, when I arrived at Phoenix College around 6:00 in the morning, it was still dark. As I passed my classroom on my way to the teachers' lounge, I would open the door and flick on the light, so it would welcome any student who arrived early.

One day after class, Martin came to the front of the room and asked if he could talk to me. Martin had never missed a class. He always sat in the back, and never participated with a question or a thought.

"Sure, Martin. I'm free now if you want," I said tapping my papers into order.

"No," he said slowly and without animation. "I've got another class now. Can I see you before class tomorrow?"

"I'll be in the teachers' lounge by 6:00. Come anytime."

He hitched his backpack onto one shoulder and turned to walk away. I wondered why he now had a peppering of dark scabs on his forehead. Not acne, the marks were curiously dark and deep, and they'd never been there before. They showed up clearly on his pale skin, his hair too short to cover them.

The Psychology Department was always unlocked by 6:00, but no other faculty ever came that early. I was in the small, windowless teachers' lounge, sitting at the corner of the table, when Martin arrived. He took the chair at right angles to mine. I put down my pen and leaned back in my chair, ready for whatever was on his mind.

Martin didn't speak. He carefully placed his backpack on the floor, and then shifted his gaze slowly from the floor to the ceiling, everywhere but at me.

I waited a bit, and then decided that if we were going to have a conversation, I was going to have to start it.

I leaned toward him. "How're you doing, Martin?"

"OK, I guess." His voice was low and flat.

"You're doing well in class. I was just grading the last test, and you've done well on all of them."

"Thanks," he said, without looking at me.

The pause lengthened.

"Is there a specific reason you wanted to see me?"

"I don't know."

"Martin," I asked gently, "why are scabs scattered across one side of your forehead? They've never been there before."

Martin sighed heavily and looked up at my face. There was no light in his eyes. He leaned his elbows on the table, and I leaned closer, to meet him halfway.

"I tried to shoot myself two nights ago—I couldn't do it. As the gun fired, I pulled it away. These are powder burns."

I felt a weight descend on my shoulders, and the light dim in the room. "Wow, things must be bad."

"Yes."

"Have you told anyone besides me? Do you live at home or with roommates?"

"I live at home."

"Do your parents know?"

"No."

"Could you tell them?"

"No."

"Martin, you know I'm a therapist, but I have a different relationship to you. I am your teacher. I assume that you told me because you want me to do something, or tell you what to do?"

"Yes."

"Well, how are you feeling right now? Can you keep yourself safe?"

"Yes, for now, but not forever."

"So, we've got to figure out who you should tell so you can get some help in staying safe. My clients are all under eighteen, and I have a duty to protect them as children. If you were under eighteen, I'd have to tell your parents."

"No, I'm twenty. You can't tell them. You can't tell anyone." For a second I saw a spark of determination in his face.

"All right, but you pulled the gun away, so at least a part of you wants to live. You say you can't keep yourself safe forever, so I'm guessing that you want to make changes in your life. You need support, but not from your parents. Do you want to see a therapist?"

"No."

"Is there any other family member that you trust?"

"I have an uncle in Minnesota."

"Could you tell him?"

"Maybe."

I'd never felt so helpless. I wasn't his therapist. I was only his teacher. I couldn't take control of his life, as I could if he had been a child. He wanted to die, but he hadn't killed himself. He'd told me about it. Clearly, he expected me to think of something.

I voiced all these thoughts and indecisions out loud to Martin. He leaned back in his chair and listened. Honesty about my uncertainties was the only control I could think of to give him.

I didn't want him to think that my lack of action about how to help him came from a lack of caring. It arose only from a lack of knowing what to do. I hoped it was a good sign that he could listen.

We talked together until it was time to go to class, but we hadn't come up with a definite plan. The uncle was still our best bet.

"Will you meet me here again tomorrow at 6:00, Martin? Can you keep yourself safe that long?"

"Yes, I'll be here."

As we walked through the department's offices to the door, the first of the other teachers began to arrive.

"Think about calling your uncle, will you, Martin?" I asked him softly as we walked along the hall to the classroom. "We have to figure out how to make your life different and better. You have to tell someone who can help you."

Martin came back the next morning, and several more mornings. Each day he renewed his pledge to stay alive. We talked about how he was doing and explored his options, but I never asked him what had made him so desperate. If I had gone down that path, it would have suggested to him that I was his therapist.

As his teacher, I had no right to ask. Martin taught me that I wanted to go back to the relatively simple world of being a therapist. Teaching reinforced for me how much I love people, but not as a teacher—as a therapist. In my therapy world, I would have had rights, too, to balance Martin's right of confidentiality. I would have had the right to pry, to assign him tasks, to consult with colleagues, to request clinical supervision, and to follow his case until I had done all I could do.

"I called my uncle," he told me on the third day.

"Did you tell him what you've been going through?"

"You mean did I tell him I tried to kill myself?"

"Yes."

"I told him everything, and he's sending me a ticket to Minnesota. He told me to come and live with him."

"Will you do that? Is that a plan you like?"

"Yes," Martin said. He picked up his backpack and turned to leave the teachers' lounge.

I felt a surge of relief. Perhaps it was because Martin's shoulders seemed a little straighter, or his voice a bit stronger. "Martin," I said, smiling at him, "your forehead is beginning to heal."

The Long Gray Room

I stepped out of the morning heat and into the cool office lobby, hurrying toward the elevator doors that stood open at the far end of the room. There were already two people in it, a man and a woman. The man held the door for me. I recognized him as I drew closer—Larry Cohen—one of the defense lawyers for counselors appearing before the Board of Behavioral Health Examiners. The Board monitors licensure and hears complaints against practitioners of the four branches of counseling: Mental Health Counseling, Social Work, Marriage and Family, and Substance Abuse. On the 9th floor of this building, the complaints were heard, the decisions made, and punishments meted out.

The woman's face was gray, and her gaze never left the elevator carpet. After Larry and I said hello, we all rode up in silence. At least she has the best lawyer, I thought, for whatever has happened to her.

I was accustomed to silent elevator rides on my way to formal hearings. If people recognized me, they were silent.

We got off at the 9th floor, and I motioned Larry and his client to go ahead. With a touch on her elbow, Larry guided her into the long room. As we entered, they turned right, to the chairs for the audience, and I turned left to sit behind the narrow table and the name plate that said Chairman of the Board.

The room was a rectangle, solid gray walls on three sides, muffling the sounds from the corridor, and tall miserly windows on the fourth side, covered with thin Venetian blinds. These allowed only angled glimpses of the outdoors and small wedges of sunlight.

Audience chairs were set in rows, and facing them, the whole length of the room away, was the dais set with tables arranged in a horseshoe, and high-back black leather chairs. The tables were empty at first, except for microphones and nameplates.

Slowly men and women filled the audience. They spoke softly to each other or sat in silence staring straight ahead.

I put my thick stack of papers—the cases we would hear today—at my place, and looked out over the audience. If I got eye contact, I smiled, but few people looked directly at me.

I had always thought that the worst job in the world was to be a judge. I had chosen a diametrically opposed career: to become a counselor, a job that does not encourage judging. Things are not measured as good or bad, but rather, as better or worse.

A counselor doesn't even have to spend much time deciding if a client is lying, although it is almost impossible to turn off that inner voice that evaluates "Truth" or "Lie" after a statement is made. Whether clients are lying or not, both are paths worth pursuing. If the statement is a factual lie, it might still be an emotional truth.

But now I was a judge, on a panel of judges, and we had to decide who was lying to us and what their fate should be. The lack of eye contact and friendly smiles was not a surprise. This was not a friendly place.

Gradually, three men and three women joined me at the high-back chairs on the dais. They acknowledged each other with smiles, but only occasionally nodded to the audience. Each carried a large stack of white paper like mine, filled with margin notes and yellow highlighting, and placed them in unsteady piles on the tables in front of them.

Four members of the board were chosen by the governor from the counseling branches to represent the standards of the profession. Three others were chosen from the public, to bring the standards of the community to the decision-making of the board. Those seven chose one among themselves to be the chairperson.

Alone, in the dead center of the room, was another long narrow table, empty except for two microphones and two chairs. They waited for people from the audience to be called up, alone or with lawyers, to face the members on the dais.

A name was called and the pale woman from the elevator stood with a jerk. As she moved from the audience to the center table, she stumbled once and touched the back of each chair she passed to steady herself. Larry Cohen moved with her, and it seemed likely she would have fallen if he hadn't held her arm. After settling her in a chair, he sat down next to her and moved a microphone in front of each of them.

I waited until they were seated and the murmurings of the audience had stopped, then said, "Please introduce yourselves for the record."

The tape recorders began to roll.

Larry leaned into his microphone and said, "My name is Larry Cohen, and I am the attorney for Sarah Platt." He looked at his companion with quiet concern, but when she neither spoke nor moved, he looked at me to continue.

"Staff," I said, "will you please read a summary of the complaint against Ms. Platt, and then you, Mr. Cohen, and you, Ms. Platt, will have an opportunity to respond."

Sarah stared at the table as a staff member read aloud, "The complainant, who was the therapy client of Sarah Platt, states that on October 12th, after an afternoon spent together at a football game, they went to have drinks and dinner at a hotel and then took a hotel room and had sex together. He states that he suffered great harm, losing confidence in his therapist, in himself, and in therapy in general."

The details of the complaint, though cut and dried, were hard to listen to, and the faces of the audience registered shock.

Having completed a summary of the client's complaint, the staff member then turned to the audience, "Is the complainant present in the room?" It was his turn in the procedure to speak for himself if he chose.

The audience rustled in their chairs, craning their necks to look around, but the complainant was not there.

I spoke into the silence. "Ms. Platt, Mr. Cohen, this is your opportunity to respond."

The lawyer turned to his client, but she did not speak. She seemed dazed, and it was unclear to me whether she could see or hear him. He turned back to his microphone, and with great gentleness, began. "My client does not deny the facts, and she takes full responsibility for what she did. However, as I am to speak for her, I would like to put these facts into their human context and ask for your leniency.

"My client," he continued, "is thirty-four years old and has been married for five years. She and her husband did not have a happy marriage, and were considering a divorce when it was discovered that he had terminal cancer, with a prognosis of only six to eight months to live. My client, Sarah, decided not to divorce her husband, but to stay and take care of him until his death.

"One of Sarah's clients," he said calmly, "the person who brought this complaint, was a successful man who came to see her because he was having trouble in his business and in his marriage.

"Ms. Platt had been nursing her husband for six months at the time she met this client, and she was depressed and vulnerable. She has instructed me to make no excuses for her, but I feel compelled to explain this. The client knew Ms. Platt's situation and invited her to an afternoon football game, telling her that she needed some distraction. After the game, he invited her for dinner at a hotel restaurant, and then persuaded Ms. Platt to stay at the hotel, telling her she had had too much to drink. One thing led to another." The lawyer's words came to a stop.

I looked at Sarah Platt's empty expression and didn't think she would reply to me, but I had my part to play. "Ms. Platt, do you have anything that you would like to add?"

A clock ticked on the wall, and the tape recorders recorded the silence. After a pause, I continued. "Then the Board will now deliberate."

The chairs rustled as board members leaned toward each other. Microphones would amplify our deliberations so the defendant and the audience could follow the thoughts leading to our decision, but there was almost nothing that any of us could say.

Why did I take this job: a combination of judge, jury, and executioner? Was it curiosity? Ambition? A naïve and arrogant belief that I could make a rigid system more flexible? But the clients, the counselors they accused, and the board members who sat in judgment, were all caught and held between the jaws of "Rules" and "Precedent." Individualized judgments were seldom given or received.

I found it easier to live with myself if I repeated over and over that I was working to create order out of chaos—that until the tangled web of crime, neglect, or betrayal had been loosened, none of the people involved could move on with their lives.

"The rules of our profession are clear," said John, a drug therapist and professor, "There is only one outcome possible. She must lose her license."

"Yes," agreed another, "but her honesty is a change from so many therapists who come before us. Most flatly deny they had sex with a client, saying the accusation was a symptom of the client's mental illness. Are we allowed to show any leniency in this case?"

"She looks as though this decision might kill her," added a member appointed from the general public, anxiously twisting her fingers together.

"We could encourage her to reapply," said a female therapist from Tucson.

"Would you reapply?" I asked them all.

"No," they murmured.

But the invitation would be offered. She was a human being after all, and so were we.

Although our deliberations had been amplified throughout the room, the verdict still needed to be stated. I looked at Sarah Platt and voiced our decision with finality. "It is the unanimous decision of this Board that Sarah Platt be ordered to surrender her license immediately."

Larry Cohen slowly pushed back his chair and helped Ms. Platt to rise. He walked her toward the door.

"It is the hope of this Board," I added loudly to their retreating backs, in hopes that she would hear me, "that after waiting the required length of time, Ms. Platt will reapply to this Board for reinstatement of her license."

Sarah Platt continued toward the door. The audience followed her with their eyes.

It was clear to everyone that she would not return.

Part VI

Family and Other Thoughts

The Jewels in My Crown

Paul and I met when we were seventeen, in our first class of our first year at Stanford.

We started dating at age nineteen, and married at twenty-one. We have three children. Michael John Bastiaan de Blank was born in 1971, Peter Matthew Kennedy de Blank in 1974, and Jennifer Gabriel Brophy de Blank (now Soden) in 1978. We were poor in the 1970s, and names were free.

I can easily remember the years of their births, but never their current ages. Whenever I'm asked how old they are I have to stop and do the arithmetic on my fingers. Usually the person who asked has drifted away before I've gotten the answers. I've learned to answer quickly, saying, "I have no idea," and then to ask accusingly, "How old are yours?"

Childraising is the ultimate cottage industry, where the final products of your labor are your new best friends. It is difficult to do these three people justice, to show them growing from children to adults, to make them three-dimensional.

Michael has been known as Bas all his life, Peter goes by Peter, and Jennifer has always been Gabriel. Two boys and a girl, strong, sturdy children who laughed, and fought, and teased each other until each, in turn, reached the requisite age to go away to boarding school, and my years of stewardship ended.

As an infant, Bas cried uninterruptedly for the first six months of his life, and it's a miracle I ever had more children. He had colic and ear infections. We had tubes put in his ears periodically throughout his early years. Looking back, maybe the miracle is that he stopped crying at six months, since he was still in pain.

Since Bas was my firstborn, everything he did was precocious and entrancing. Due to his ear infections, his speech was distorted, so he and I developed a secret language. This was convenient, when at age two he decided to explain the difference between men and women to me. Sitting in the grocery cart while we waited in line at the cash register, he pointed his pudgy little finger at all the men and women he could see. "I've got it, Mom," he repeated over and over. "He's got a penis and she doesn't."

Bas is humorous. His first real joke came at age five. We were driving together and he had his bag of Halloween candy on his lap. Suddenly, all the candy started to spill out on the floor at his feet.

"Oh," I said, "Do you have a hole in your bag?"

"Only the one at the top," he replied.

As a child, he loved the infinite potential of plastic lizards and insects. He never tired of tucking his white toy lizard in the sun visor of the car, then waiting for days or weeks for me to drive into the sun and lower the visor. The lizard would fall into my lap, and I would shriek, "Bas!!!"

He'd leave plastic spiders on the cradle of the telephone so that when I lifted the receiver, the spider would stare back at me.

He would suddenly shout, "GO!" while we were stopped at a red light.

I learned from him not to believe everything I was told. Most days, I screamed, snorted, laughed, and snarled at him. Possibly giving him a mixed message.

When he was in his first year of high school, his last year at home, I received a telephone call one afternoon from a voice I didn't recognize.

"Hello," said the adolescent male voice, "you don't know me, but I'm one of Bas's friends at school. I'm calling to tell you that he was just caught shoplifting from Circle K, and has been arrested."

This seemed odd. I'd never known Bas to steal anything, nor was he stupid.

"What did he steal?" I asked.

"A two-liter bottle of Coke," came the reply.

"Nonsense," I said. "Go play your silly tricks on someone else. My son Bas would never steal a two-liter bottle of Coke. It is far too big for him to get away with it."

That was the same year I had to take Bas to the interview at his prospective boarding school. I hoped he'd get in if that was what he wanted, but losing him was so painful that I made my husband take Peter and Gabriel to the interviews when their turns came. It was Paul's idea that they'd get a better education in boarding school, not mine. He'd never been away to boarding school himself, and he had an image of it as a scholastic Garden of Eden.

Boarding schools are not Gardens of Eden. Teachers do not sit at dinner with you as Paul imagined, having stimulating conversations about world affairs. But Bas seemed to enjoy it. He has an unflappable temperament that is a good match for just about everything life can throw at you, certainly for the trials of boarding school.

During Bas's interview at Milton Academy, the Dean of Admissions took me into his office alone, and solemnly asked me to tell him about Bas. I thought a moment and then said, "What stands out for me about Bas is that he is trustworthy. I would trust him with the life of a newborn baby, or with my deepest secret. He's young, but he would do his utmost."

The Dean looked surprised and didn't respond. He just jotted notes in his folder.

Bas called us from school one evening in November of his first year to tell us about an exciting incident. He explained that the day before, he had been watching television in the common room, when a senior boy had asked him if he would like to help refill the new soda cans into the vending machine.

I blame myself for what happened next. Clearly I hadn't taught Bas the difference between a real question and a polite command. Now that I think back on it, I always had to rephrase my questions into commands, too, when there were chores to be done.

Bas made the mistake of thinking this was a request, so he said, "No, thanks, I'm busy right now."

The senior didn't say anything then, but in the middle of the night, four upperclassmen, their faces obscured by ski masks, burst into Bas's room, flicking on the ceiling light, roaring that he and his roommate, Julian, should respect their elders and betters. The marauders pounded the boys with pillows. Bas and Julian were outnumbered and thoroughly pounded. Eventually satisfied, the upperclassmen left.

When the room was quiet again, and Bas and his roommate continued lying in their beds, staring at each other and watching the occasional pillow feather drift to the floor, Bas explained to Julian that this was perhaps in retaliation for the soda machine decision he had made, which wasn't entirely fair for his roommate. Julian was just saying, "That's quite all right," when Bas noticed a knit cap on the floor, and since it was very cold outside, he figured the owner would be back.

Sure enough, within minutes, the door opened again—not quite so forcefully—and a single masked boy re-entered. Bas simply held out the hat, and the boy took it with a word of thanks.

Bas worked hard to raise his sister Gabriel, in spite of the fact that her father and I were standing right there. He worried that Paul and I were becoming increasingly sloppy in our childrearing responsibilities.

"You're letting that child eat on the couch again," he'd scold. "You know the rule is that all food must be eaten in the kitchen!"

"Yes, Bas," I agreed, "that was certainly the rule when you were young, but back then I was younger, too, and so was the couch."

As a young man, Bas wrote us an email about a dream he'd had that continued to reflect his concerns.

Dear Mother and Father,

Well, I hope you are happy. I had a dream that we were all flying back from India and you had let Gabriel take home a baby elephant (which was currently in the overhead compartment).

Once again, I was the only sane family member who thought that perhaps this was not a good idea and that the elephant would not be happy for the entire flight.

Anyway, you two were sitting together in the back of the plane and I had to go get some more hay for it (since, obviously, none of the rest of you could be trusted to care for it properly). You had brought one small bag of hay (which I, at least, could tell would not be nearly enough for the entire flight) and when I tried to raise some concerns about the course of action, all either of you could talk about was how excited the dogs would be with their new friend. Anyway, I took half the hay back and returned to my seat while the attendant was taking lunch orders.

I almost got into a fight with Peter who did not want a sandwich (I wanted him to order one so we could give the elephant the bread at least) and he did not understand what I was talking about (I did not want to come right out and say we had a baby elephant in the overhead bin, as I doubted the stewardess would approve.) Anyway, I finally convinced him to do so and the stewardess left and all I could think about was that it was not going to be easy taking an elephant through customs.

All I can say is that this is what your laissez faire child rearing has brought us to.

If Gabriel had asked me, I never would have let

her bring home an elephant.
I will talk to you later.

Bas

When Bas graduated from law school, he asked me whether I was coming to his graduation ceremony.

"But you'll have already left for your job in California," I said.

"That's not the point," he said. "The mothers of all the other little boys will be there."

*   *   *   *

Peter seemed like an easy baby compared to Bas. He had fine blond hair that stuck straight out from his head, making him resemble a baby bird.

Peter spent much of his childhood fighting with Bas over who got the red cup or the yellow plate, which bedtime story to hear, which TV show to watch, what to eat for dinner, whose turn it was to take out the trash, and whether or not there was enough air on our planet for them both. It was a full rich life for them and provided the mutual satisfaction of driving their mother mad.

A good student, Peter won every prize but one at his elementary school graduation. He was called up to the podium over and over, until it came time for the Spanish prize, which was won by the son of the Spanish teacher. I think even Peter was relieved.

Being a good student doesn't mean you know everything. Like his brother and sister, Peter spent his freshman year of high school in Phoenix, then went away to boarding school starting with his sophomore year.

As a Brophy Prep freshman, he took fencing as a sport. He liked the cool white uniform and thought of himself as Luke Skywalker fighting the bad guys with a light saber.

When the coach sent home a list of necessary supplies at the beginning of the fencing season, I took Peter shopping for the jock strap and cup. We went to a sporting goods store, and stood side by side studying the athletic supporters hanging on hooks against the wall. Peter took down a package and read the information on the back. He nudged me and whispered, "There's only large and medium up there, Mom, and according to this size chart, I'm a small."

I saw a cute young salesgirl in the sneaker aisle and asked her if they had a small athletic supporter and cup in the storeroom. She went off to look, and I turned to speak to Peter, but he was no longer there. I found him hiding behind a pyramid of basketballs.

"Why are you over here?" I asked.

"It wouldn't matter if I needed a large," he whispered. "But a small!"

The salesgirl found our item, and we proceeded to the cash register. Because the jock strap had just come from the storeroom, it hadn't been priced. So the cashier grabbed her microphone and asked for a price check.

Her voice boomed throughout the store in a disinterested monotone. "Would someone tell me the price of the Athletic Supporter and cup in size small?"

Peter had already left to sit in the car.

At the beginning of his first practice, the coach told the boys to put on their cups, without explaining how. So Peter shoved it down the front of his pants, under his jock strap but outside his briefs. Then he went out to the school hallway where the fencing took place—this being a very low-budget sport for his school. He began to fence against another freshman boy, lunging, parrying, and generally having a good time.

When Peter got home from school, he sat at the kitchen counter eating an apple and told me about the match.

"And then, Mom, I made a great leap forward, but I'd been able to feel that cup creeping down my pant leg ever since the beginning, and when I kicked out my leg, it shot out my pant cuff. It hit my opponent right in the chest!"

"Good heavens," I said, leaning my elbows on the counter in front of him. "Then what happened?"

"Oh, I just told the other boy that it didn't matter if it was the foil or the cup. It was a direct hit, and he had to concede the match."

When Peter did go away to boarding school, he was bitterly homesick for his first year. He could forget his misery in his studies, so he kept his grades up. I kept telling him to come home, that this amount of misery wasn't worth it, but he kept on going back after each vacation, refusing to give up. By the second year, he had adjusted, and once again began to hold all the student offices and win all the prizes.

With Peter in his senior year of boarding school, Gabriel was almost ready to go away to a boarding school herself. That Christmas vacation, as the whole family was eating out at a Mexican restaurant, we got to talking about what school Gabriel might choose. We sat at the scarred wooden booth, heaping plates of enchiladas and burritos in front of us, and Peter said, "You know, since Gabriel is the youngest, when she goes, you and Dad will be all alone. Maybe she'd better stay home and not go away to school."

I saw the wide-eyed look of panic on Gabriel's face as she waited in silence to see whether she would be stuck at home forever, taking care of aging parents.

"It's kind of you, Peter, to worry about us," I replied, taking a sip of iced tea. "But if you think we should have a child at home, perhaps it should be you. You've had two years away at school, so you could come home and Gabriel could have a turn away."

Peter looked at us for a minute, dipped his forkful of burrito in some salsa, and said, "No, I guess you guys will be fine."

After college and before medical school, Peter returned to his boarding school, Concord Academy, as a teacher, first of sophomore and AP Chemistry, and later of English literature, as well.

After working and saving money for four years, Peter entered medical school at the University of California at San Francisco in September of 2001.

Four years later, Paul and I went to San Francisco to celebrate Peter's graduation. Peter was selected to give the commencement address, which I've excerpted below, about the process of becoming a doctor, starting with his first patient: Annie the first-aid mannequin.

> When I opened the door, I found Annie lying on the ground. She wasn't moving, her mouth formed in an "O" of surprise. I touched her shoulder and said, "Annie, Annie, are you OK?"
>
> Annie was my first patient at UCSF. She had no past, no complications with a co-dependent girlfriend, no pain killer addiction spurred on by chronic back pain. And we were asked to save her.
>
> I surveyed the situation: things didn't look good. Annie hadn't breathed spontaneously since I entered the room. Her skin felt plastic. And, most remarkably, she had lost both arms and both legs in some unknown previous mishap.
>
> Annie never really had a chance. Apart from her formidable health problems, her best available health care was from medical students with one week of experience. We were former schoolteachers, consultants, and Peace Corps volunteers. We could field a champion volleyball team or a professional

orchestra. One of us worked on a nuclear submarine. We wore our starched white coats and hung our new stethoscopes around our necks, but we were not doctors.

I was floundering to save Annie. I forgot to lock my elbows over her chest, and my compressions were too weak to pump her blood. Annie never complained.

Nor did the next hundred real patients. Somehow, all those patients knew we were learning. They took our stumbling with humor, patience, and, occasionally, with pity. Then they let us try again.

Medicine is taught through experience, and the best lessons are learned from patients. We care for patients and soon reach the limits of our understanding, and that's where we start to learn. You can't teach these skills from a book. We make a thousand mistakes in order to earn that first success. And we make many more to refine our skills, our judgment, our practice of medicine.

I hate mistakes. I've spent the majority of my life trying to avoid making mistakes. We have earned our entrance into medical school, in part, by our ability to make fewer mistakes than the next person. And now, medicine is telling us that we must make mistakes in order to learn. Each has a lesson to teach.

Next year, we move on to internship: to new mistakes and new lessons. I'll wish us the best of mistakes. The ones that train intuition and demonstrate humanity. And most of all, the willingness to rise from mistakes willing to make more.

Peter and his wife Robin are the parents of two little girls now, and he has learned a lot about raising females. I told him on the phone the other day that I'd been to the movies that afternoon, and when I had gone to the ladies room before heading home, I had heard a little girl of about four in the stall next to mine calling, "Dad! Daddy!" over and over. She had left her stall door open by a few inches, so I went to her and asked where her daddy was.

"Just outside the door," she replied.

"Well, I don't think it will help to call him, as he is a man and this place is just for girls, so do you want me to help you?"

"Yes," she said.

I told Peter I'd wiped her bottom, washed her hands, and opened the heavy door of the ladies' room, and that her father had been pacing just outside. I didn't tell Peter that I had been thinking uncharitable thoughts about a father who would let a little girl go into a restroom alone, but perhaps he sensed my thoughts.

He gave me his take on the probable activity behind the scene I had witnessed.

"Oh, yes," said Peter, "I know that scenario well. The girl had probably told her father in no uncertain terms that she was far too old to go into the men's room with him anymore, and would go to the ladies room all by herself!"

"Well, in that case," I replied, "she should probably learn how to wipe herself before going off on her own."

"Ah, yes," said Peter knowingly, "and that's the conversation her father had with her as soon as he got her back."

Peter continued, "I'm sure the father put up a fight at first, telling his daughter she couldn't go in alone. And she said, 'But I've really, really gotta pee,' and he said, 'But you can't go alone…. No wait, there's a grandmotherly woman going in now.' And giving her a little shove, he said, 'Go, go, go, go!'"

*   *   *   *

Gabriel is our last child and our first girl. It was lucky that she was number three, because Paul said we had to keep on having children until he got a girl, and if she hadn't come when she did this essay might be even longer.

Bas named Gabriel. He was a shepherd in the school's Christmas pageant that year, and came home from rehearsal saying, "If it's a girl we should name her Gabriel."

Since we were having trouble deciding on a name for a girl baby, as most female names had been ruined for me by my elementary school classmates, we grabbed the idea. We didn't feminize it to Gabrielle, as she is named directly after the Archangel. There is always the hope that people may think it is an old family name, and that the Archangel is one of our ancestors.

Gabriel and Peter continued the battle over who got the red cup or the yellow plate. Bas was getting too old for that by the time she came along and had cheerfully passed on the baton of sibling rivalry to his brother. This time around, Peter won all the arguments, while Gabriel fought as furiously as he once had.

Possibly due to this early training, Gabriel is both fierce and nurturing. One afternoon when she was nine, she demanded to be left at home while I watched Peter's baseball game. The game ended early due to a mighty hailstorm battering us from an orange-gray sky. I had to pull the car over on our way home because the hail was so heavy and the wind so powerful I couldn't see to drive.

When we finally arrived, parking the car in the driveway, Peter and I rushed toward the house to be sure Gabriel was OK. As I neared the wrought-iron gate, I could see her at the other end of the breezeway, dressed in her raincoat, sitting cross-legged on the cement with our two large dogs, one on either side of her, her arms protectively around their waists. All three were looking out toward the backyard, watching the storm rage.

"Gabriel, why aren't you three inside where it's safe?" I called to her.

"Oh, hi, Mom," she shouted over the sound of the wind and the hail. "The wind blew the patio umbrella into the French doors and broke one of the panes. There's glass all over the rug in the TV room. I couldn't clean it up with the dogs in the house, because they would have cut their paws on it, and I couldn't put them outside alone or they would have been scared, so we all came out. We're fine."

Gabriel took full advantage of her position as the only girl. She felt that, since she was the only one of our children who hadn't run afoul of the law in some way, she deserved some special recognition, preferably monetary.

Gabriel would have made a good lawyer if she hadn't become a psychologist. In addition to wanting to be rewarded for a crime-free life, or at least for not getting caught, she also wanted to negotiate all rules. At the age of twelve, she demanded to know what her curfew would be when she reached sixteen. What the significance of sixteen was I have no idea, but then I often didn't understand the conversations I had with my children.

"Well, your curfew depends on where you would be going," I stalled.

"That is entirely irrelevant!" she countered.

"No, it's not. If you're going to a school dance then your curfew might be midnight, but if you're just roaming the streets with your friends, then your curfew would be whenever dark falls."

"That's so unfair! My brothers have never had any curfews!" she shouted, springing her trap.

"Ah, yes," I replied, happily realizing that I wasn't just a sexist mother with a hopelessly double standard, "but your brothers have never actually gone anywhere."

Conversations with my children were often what Gabriel calls "ships that pass in the night." I thought that I knew my children. After all, I'd created them and lived with them for years. But as they grew into adults, I had to keep reminding myself they were their own people, not mine any longer.

During Gabriel's freshman year of college, Paul and I went up to Reed in Portland to visit her for Parents' Weekend. As she and I walked along a campus sidewalk, she told me that her favorite blue teapot-teacup combination had gotten broken during the move.

"Oh, that's too bad," I said. "I saw one in a store recently. I'll send you a replacement."

Gabriel narrowed her eyes. "That is just so typical of you, Mother. You think that every problem can be solved with money. That teapot had great sentimental value to me. It can't just be replaced!"

I paused, not knowing exactly how to respond to this attack. "But," I murmured tentatively, "I was the one who gave you that blue teapot originally."

"Oh," Gabriel replied. "No, this was another teapot."

We walked on in silence.

Last week, when I sent two essays that concerned them to my three children so they could correct any mistakes I'd made, I got this email back from Gabriel:

> Hi Mom,
>
> Those are lovely essays, thanks for sending them on. They are great and there is no need to change anything. However, I would just mention to you that we may have been ships passing in the night about that blue teapot incident, so I thought I would try to clarify. It really was a different teapot. A senior at Milton named Kit had "willed" it to me on the eve of her graduation back when I was a sophomore (a big tradition there).
>
> I had been depressed and scared those first weeks at Milton and one day she asked me how I was doing, and when I shook my head and started to cry, she took me back to her room and made me tea.

Months later I thanked her for being so kind and told her how much it had meant to me, and she had answered that it's so easy to be kind and doesn't cost anything at all. So then, when she mentioned me (a lowly sophomore) in her will, and gave me the teapot, I felt like I had something important to live up to and a goal for the kind of person I wanted to become.

So when I had a horrible senior year at Milton and experienced what felt like a lot of cruelty from my peers that spring, and then got to Reed and was doing pretty miserably there too, and found that this teapot, which had represented something to me about the qualities of kindness in others, had been broken, well, I felt like it was a literal reminder that a part of me, and what I wanted the world to be like, was broken too. And it was all the worse because it was my own fault things were broken; I had carelessly left it unwrapped in my mini fridge and it had gotten banged around.

I am sort of surprised that I had tried to tell you about the teapot that fall because it felt really personal and raw to me at the time, and I'm sure I didn't do a very good job of explaining it. But I can see why, if I had tried and felt that your response was to just buy another, I might have snapped at you and felt misunderstood. And probably frustrated to have you think that it was to do with you. I would have been irritated that I couldn't communicate these things to you without you seeing the issue as a quick and easy fix, when it felt like so much more to me.

I just had to explain that because in the story it sounds like you thought it really was a teapot from you and that I was just picking a fight. That wasn't what was happening in my head; I had been trying to share something with you. But I'm sure it's just one example, and maybe many other times I was just picking a fight. So, while it's not my truth, it may be yours, and you have every right to write about it that way. No need to change anything, I just wanted you to know all of that.

Gabriel

After college and before her doctorate, Gabriel joined the Peace Corps and was sent to Ghana for two years and three months. She was a Water and Sanitation Volunteer and worked hard to get her village running water and clean latrines in all the schools. She found a grant from the Danish government that would have paid for pipes to go from the well along the streets of the village, so each house would have had a spigot outside their front door, but the village chieftain and the elders couldn't raise the 5% match. Denmark would pay $200,000, but the village would have to come up with $10,000. They tried hard, contacting every villager and even those who had left, but they couldn't do it. Gabriel got funding for more wells, a catchment system, and latrines, but they had to keep going to the well for water.

Gabriel learned Twi, the language of southern Ghana and did a lot of AIDS prevention work through lectures, conferences, and even a musical play she wrote with the high school kids, about healthy living through condoms. They rented a little van and performed their play at other high schools.

It wasn't easy staying sane in the Peace Corps. There is enormous isolation and culture shock. Most of the villagers had never seen a white person, an "obruni," before. One old woman came up to Gabriel as she sat at the well, and putting her hands on Gabriel's breasts said, "Oh, you have them too."

In one of her emails from Ghana, Gabriel wrote:

> It's becoming harder and harder to think of things to write for these emails. I mean, exotic and sanity-challenging events occur every day, but they don't seem so noteworthy to me and I'm not sure I so much want to parade my life around as one long anecdote. Everything's so exhausting too—I don't know where to start.
>
> Yesterday I did some market shopping and realized I thought my pocket with my keys was empty. I was so tired that rather than look on the ground around me I figured I'd just ride the 45 minutes home in the bus without moving and hope they showed up or that I could break into my house. I just couldn't deal with anything right then. I was too wiped out even to pat my pocket—which shows you where I'm at because there they were, of course.
>
> I'm a bit sick too, which in the best of

circumstances slows me down but right now it
throws a steaming wet blanket over me and pummels
me and steals my IQ points and apparently then my
keys. At least it returned the keys.

In fact, I jumped out of a bus the other day to
crouch by the bumper and vomit and there I was all
nasty and sick and someone kept nudging me trying
to sell me something. I felt like death and finally
looked up with glassy eyes and a line of drool down
my chin to tell him to leave and he said, "I think you
want to buy this." And he held out a toothbrush.

Thanks so much, buddy.

Gabriel's tour of duty improved with time, but she still marked off
the days by moving a bookmark through a thick book of
approximately 800 pages.

Bas, Peter, and Gabriel are grown now and scattered across the
country. Bas is an intellectual property litigator in California, Peter is
a pediatric neuro-oncologist in Ohio, and Gabriel is a psychologist
with a community mental health center in Massachusetts. Each one is
married, with children of their own. They have valuable careers, and
they work hard. They call us, laughing, and when they forget, we call
them.

They still tease each other and Paul and me. I love watching them
raise their own children. They are all better and more patient parents
than I was. But they couldn't have more fun with their kids than I did,
or love them any more than I do.

Peter, Gabriel, and Bas, 2002

A Long Friendship with Heaven at the End of It

The children were grown and gone, and Paul and I filled our life with our careers, our friends, ideas, dreams, and each other.

"It's Nancy for you," Paul said, handing me the phone. It was early for a call. We were still in our pajamas in the kitchen, drinking coffee and trading parts of the newspaper.

Nancy started speaking before I could get the phone to my ear, her words coming out in short bursts. "Jon is asking for you, Laura. The doctors say he won't make it through the night. Come quickly." Jon was eighty-five, but the end from cancer was coming sooner than anticipated.

"I'll leave right away. Tell him I'm coming." I hung up and ran to the bedroom, pulling my pajama top over my head on the way.

Paul drove me to the airport, pushing through every yellow light and passing every truck, while I talked to Southwest Airlines, trying to get to Portland, Oregon. I gripped my cell phone so tightly that it became slippery with sweat. It took forever to arrange the series of flights that would get me there, and toward the end of the call, the agent said, "Well, you can't get on the 9 AM flight now, because that leaves in half an hour, and security rules require that you book a flight at least an hour before it leaves."

"Well, it was 8 when we started this conversation," I snarled.

The ticket agent saw my point, and also how to get a surly woman off the phone. She agreed to get me a stand-by reservation on the 9 o'clock.

As Paul unloaded my bag from the car, I hugged him extra hard for putting up with a stressed wife, and for being the best husband any woman ever had.

"Say hi to Jon from me," he said.

"I will, and I'll call you tonight."

I waited on the hard plastic chairs of several airports for three stand-by flights and a taxi ride.

Jon had taught the first psychology class I took at Phoenix College. I signed up because it had been fourteen years since I'd been an undergraduate. I wanted to find out if my brain still worked before applying to a master's of counseling program. If I did this, I'd have to study with a house full of children. I'd have to think about more complicated topics than the relative merits of Pampers and Huggies.

I took psychology courses for two years at Phoenix College, catching up on undergraduate subjects I needed, and waiting for the children to get old enough for me to start grad school. Jon taught several of those classes, and wrote a letter of recommendation for me to get into ASU.

The "old friend network" benefitted me. Jon was chair of the Psychology Department at Phoenix College. He hired me to supervise the Statistics lab, and later, after I had finished the master's, gave me a job teaching two sections of Psychology 101. I had a 7 o'clock and an 8 o'clock class, and I taught them three mornings a week for ten years, before starting my day at Tumbleweed.

Jon and I worked together for ten years and remained good friends for thirty. I ate lunch with him every week, as he mentored me through academic and workplace challenges. In 2004, he moved from Phoenix to Seattle. Our lunches were replaced by phone calls.

The taxi dropped me off at the Ashland Community Hospital. I walked through the sliding glass doors, took the elevator to the third floor, and walked down the dimly lit, disinfectant-smelling corridor to Jon's room.

I stopped for a moment in the doorway, looking at the bright lights, white sheets, and slanted venetian blinds that cut the setting sun into slices. His wife Nancy stood in the center of the room talking to a nurse. Jon was lying, pale and still, in the narrow bed in the center of the room. His eyes were half closed, and he vocalized an animal sound of patience and hopelessness on each exhalation. "Huuunh.... Huuunh...." It was a sharp contrast to the man I had known. The handsome man with a deep voice and a twinkle in his eye.

Nancy saw me, and in response to my questioning look toward Jon, she said, "He says he makes that noise to comfort himself."

As I approached Jon's bed, I touched first the lump his foot made under the covers, then his leg.

Nancy spoke louder and pointed her words at her husband. "Oh look, Jon, here's your little buddy, Laura."

I kept my eyes on Jon, but registered her words. "Little buddy," like hell.

I took his hand. Though the IV was still in place, the drip line had been removed. I put my head close to his and said, "Hi, Jon, I'm here."

He stopped saying "huuunh" to listen.

I added, "We've got to stop meeting like this."

Reaching for my face and letting his hand slide down my cheek, he said, "People are starting to talk."

I smoothed his hair back, running my hand over the crisp gray curls.

Nancy asked me to step out into the hall for a minute.

I gave Jon's hand a squeeze and said, "I'll be right back."

As soon as I joined her, she said, "Would you think me awful if I went home now that you're here? I just can't stand any more of this. Is that bad?"

"No," I said, looking up and studying the spot where the gray wall met the white tiled ceiling. "Go home and rest. We don't know how long his dying will take, and if you get stressed you'll get sick."

She touched my arm lightly. "The armchair next to his bed folds out into a bed," she said. "You'll be able to sleep comfortably."

"I'll be fine." Then, as she turned to walk away, I had a thought. "Do you want me to call you if he dies in the night?"

She turned back to face me. "Yes, I suppose so, although if it's after midnight, maybe just wait until 6:00."

I nodded, and with that she was gone, me staring after her.

I had just asked Nancy if she wanted to be called if her husband died, and she had responded with the equivalent of "No, I'm good."

I returned to Jon's room and sat in the armchair near his head. I took his hand, and we settled in together.

"Where will you stay tonight?" he asked.

"Right here in the chair next to you."

Jon had once told me that his father had been frightened of dying. I had asked him, "Frightened of what?" Jon had replied slowly, "Of leaving the known for the unknown, I think."

I decided to tell him about my view of heaven, or at least the journey there, as my mother had explained it to me.

"When it's your time to die," I said, holding his hand, "you'll find yourself standing on the platform of a tree-shaded country station on a summer afternoon. You'll hear the whistle of a locomotive coming closer. Around the bend will come an old-fashioned, English steam engine, pulling three or four passenger cars. It will pull to a stop in front of you, with a screech of its wheels and a loud pssst of escaping steam. Up and down the train cars, windows will be thrown open, and your friends and family will stick their heads out to greet you with shouts of joy."

Jon smiled. I took this as permission to continue.

"They've all come from heaven to accompany you. Maybe it will be

173

your older brother who'll show you to your compartment. As the train pulls out, he'll place the books you've brought on the seat, and put your small suitcase into the overhead rack.

"Soon, your friend Bruce will stick his head in the door and tell you it's time for dinner, then take you to the dining car. There, you'll sit at a table with white linen napkins and a bud vase of spring freesias. You'll dine on corned beef sandwiches with mustard, and black coffee, and talk and laugh with all your friends. Occasionally, you'll look out the window at the night scene flashing past, but mostly you'll see a reflection in the window pane of the warmth and color within."

Jon didn't say anything in response. Speaking was becoming difficult. But he nodded slightly. His train wasn't far away. I determined that he wouldn't be scared if I could help it.

I made up the chair/bed with sheets the nurse brought me, turned off the lights, and tried to reach up to hold his hand. The metal edge of his bed cut into my forearm, stopping the circulation, so I sat up in the chair and slid my hand, palm down, under his back, letting his weight pin my hand to him if I fell asleep.

In the night he woke. "Laura?"

"Yes, Jon, I'm here," I said, reaching for his hand.

He said into the dark, "Will you know what to do?" His voice was a rasp.

"Yes," I shifted closer, "if you need help, I'll go down the hall for the nurse."

"No, that's not it." He paused for breath. "Will you know what to do?" His mind and words got caught in a loop then, and he began to repeat the same question over and over. "Will you know what to do?"

Suddenly, I realized what he was asking. Would I know what to do to help his wife and three adult children after his death: Nancy, who would be a new widow, his daughter, who would miss him dreadfully, his older son with his tightrope walk between chronic pain and addiction, and his younger son with two small children and a looming divorce. Here was Jon's fear of the unknown, not for himself but for his family.

God no, I thought, I won't have a clue. But as Jon's words escalated into agitation, I said the only thing I could say. "Yes, I'll know what to do." God help me.

With that, he relaxed and went back to sleep.

He was still alive in the morning, but completely blind now, and no longer speaking. I knew he was awake when he began vocalizing "huuunh" on the exhale again. If he needed comfort, I'd do my best. I talked to him of how his family would support each other, of how I would help, of how he was leaving them a legacy of knowing he had thoroughly loved them, of the lovely morning that was dawning, of the color and warmth of the autumn day, of long enchanted train rides, and the loved ones who would take him to Heaven.

When I ran out of words I began to sing him every song I knew.

Christmas Roller Coaster, 2014

Perhaps the meaning of Christmas is to remind us that both hope and disappointment exist—in equal balance if we are very lucky. The Christmas lights that hang from the eaves of our house are a metaphor for the season. They come in a variety of colors: red, green, blue, yellow, and an odd shade of purple. When lit at night, they create a magical glow, and in the daytime they are a dusty string of reality, especially in June. Their daytime appearance is just as real as their nighttime one. A chronological journal of our Christmas holidays shows my emotional roller coaster ride.

Back to the Beginning: December 21

Our son Bas, his wife Michelle, and their children Elijah, eleven, and Paisley, nine, arrive. This is the year that all three of our grown children and their families will return to their old home for Christmas.

Paul and I move from our bedroom into the small guest room behind our garage. Paul loves this room and is delighted that the overcrowding in the house requires us to move out there.

"It's as good as a vacation!" he extolls.

The guest bed is only a double, and we have to spoon our bodies together to keep from kicking each other onto the floor. Turning over requires the advanced planning and long practice of Can Can dancers. There is no room in bed for the dogs, who look hurt as they stare up at us from their dog beds. The cat has to sleep on top of me, and makes threatening noises when I move.

"That is not how it works," I tell the cat.

December 22

Our daughter Gabriel and her family, husband Pete, son Aengus, six, daughter Maeve, four, and son Cullen, six months, call to say that Cullen has been diagnosed with pneumonia. They have to cancel their trip to us.

I sit on the kitchen stool feeling sad. With the joy of anticipation, I'd made all the beds, constructed the Pack 'n Play, retrieved the bikes and roller skates from the storage locker, wrapped the stocking presents and the tree presents, and had visions of Elijah and Paisley teaching Aengus and Maeve how to play the dreidel game. I will miss them.

Paul suggests that they postpone, instead of cancel, hoping Cullen will be well enough to fly in a day or two, so they rebook for the 24th.

Aengus the Shepherd, Maeve the Angel, and Cullen the Christ Child at their church pageant the week before Christmas

December 23

Paisley has thought up a Christmas secret of her own. She plans on giving her American Girl doll to her cousin Maeve. She knows I am giving American Girl dolls to her cousins Casey and Reed, and wants Maeve to be able to play dolls with them when they are together. Paisley had gathered up all her doll's outfits collected over the years, brushed its hair carefully into two pig tails and tied them with silver-belled hair elastics, and brought the doll with her to Phoenix for Maeve.

December 24

Peter and Gabriel Soden

Gabriel calls again on December 24th. "We all got kicked off the plane, Mom, so we won't be coming to Phoenix for Christmas after all."

"Good grief," I replied, trying to sound calm. "What happened?"

"Pete, and I, and all three kids were seated in the plane, with our seat belts buckled, waiting for take-off when the flight attendant heard us talking about how the baby had been sick with pneumonia. I showed her the doctor's notes saying he was well enough to travel, and Pete told her that he is a doctor, but it didn't make any difference. She kicked us off."

"We'll have Christmas at home, Mom," she says through tears. "Would you please send the Christmas presents to Boston as fast as you can?"

*   *   *   *

We call our son Peter and his wife Robin and daughters Casey, six, and Reed, four, in Cleveland. They are having Christmas at their house and will all get on a plane and come to us on the 26th.

Peter tells me that, wanting each child to have lots of packages to unwrap, he has been wrapping everything he could find. He wrapped a single pair of socks for Casey and cleverly signed it from "Your Sockret Admirer." When Casey sees the lumpy little package under the tree, she is enchanted.

"Oh, it's from my secret admirer! Who do you suppose that could be?"

"I don't know," says her father. "Who do you think?"

"It must be from someone my age," announces Casey, "because whoever wrote the card can't spell secret."

"Oh," says Peter, feeling a bit out of his depth. "Well, it might be from just about anyone."

Casey continues to carry her wrapped package around with her all Christmas Eve, filled with delightful anticipation. Peter begins to get more and more worried about her eventual disappointment over a pair of socks.

At bedtime on Christmas Eve, Casey climbs into bed with her parents still clutching her package.

"What do you think is in there?" asks her father.

"I know what it is," she replies, feeling the soft lumpy parcel. "It's an MP3 player!"

"I can't stand this any longer," announces Peter. "I am your 'Sockret Admirer.'"

"Oh," she pauses, and then says "Well, that's wonderful, Dad. I'd love to have you as my sockret admirer."

"And about what's in it," he continues. "You see the word sockret? What word does that look like?"

"Secret? Rocket?"

"No, no," he wails, "the word 'sock' is in it. It's just a joke about an admirer giving you socks."

"You mean there are socks in this package?"

"Yes," he replies, unable to meet her gaze.

"That's great, Dad," she smiles at him. "I love socks."

*   *   *   *

Back in Phoenix, Paul and Bas cook wonderful food: beef tenderloin for Christmas Eve and smoked turkey on Christmas day.

Bas, Paisley, Michelle, and Elijah

Michelle and I sit at the kitchen table rehearsing with Elijah and Paisley how to say polite things when they open their gifts. We suggest "Oh, thank you!" or "Just what I wanted!" or "How beautiful!" as opposed to their more spontaneous comments of "What is this?" or "Why did you give this to me?"

December 25

On Christmas morning, Elijah and Paisley do wonderfully well and make lots of happy grateful noises.

Gabriel calls to wish us Merry Christmas and update us. She tells us that she and Pete have explained everything to Aengus and Maeve. "You see, Santa has already planned his route and your presents will be delivered to Phoenix, but Oma will send them on by mail in a few days. There will just be a few things under the tree, perhaps that Santa can drop down the chimney as he flies overhead." Once she hangs up, Gabriel leaves the kids with Pete, and rushes off to shop at Target.

On Christmas morning, after a night where the parents get up every two hours to give Cullen his breathing treatments, Maeve runs into their room shouting, "Mommy! Daddy! Santa did come and he brought thousands and thousands of presents!"

Christmas at the Soden household spreads over days as the packages from Phoenix arrive one by one. The present Aengus really wants, the one he asked Santa for in his letter—the Pokemon cards—arrives in the fifth and final box on January 2nd.

Before that gift finally arrives, Aengus had become so desperate that he had started a threatening letter to Santa.

Dear Santa,

I don't like you any more....

*   *   *   *

December 26

Peter, Robin, Casey, and Reed arrive in Phoenix, and open the presents we have kept for them here.

December 27–30

The days between Christmas and New Year's pass quickly. The small girls, Casey and Reed, run round and round the house shrieking with delight at life in general. Elijah and Paisley are older, so their voices are lower and they have a bit more gravitas, but their level of excitement is the same. Elijah teaches them to play the dreidel game.

From time to time, I retreat into my study with a stiff drink to play a game of Spider Solitaire on my computer.

Lunch out—Laura, Casey, Robin, Paul, Reed, and Peter

December 31

Peter and his family leave for Cleveland, and Bas and his family go to Palo Alto.

Paul and I move back into our bedroom. Our dogs jump onto the bed and lie down, giving us long, territorial looks. The cat narrows his eyes, and settling down, seems to murmur, "Whatever…."

My house has returned to normal, now that I have sent five boxes of gifts to Gabriel and her family, as well as three boxes to Bas and his family, of things they forgot or that didn't fit in their suitcases. The lady at the post office knows me by name and asks how Cullen is doing.

Gabriel says that after delivering all those boxes, her mail lady hates her.

Paul and I have survived the Christmas season. We're still married to each other, and our children and grandchildren are still speaking to us.

The string of decorative lights hanging from the eaves has been lit more often than it has been unlit in the last two weeks, if you know when to look for it.

A Photograph of the Future, 2015

In July, a photographer will immortalize
The marriage of my nephew D'Arcy to Vivien.
I want him to turn briefly
From the inner-lit smiles of bride and groom
To point his camera at my offshoot of the family tree.

This wedding will be the first time our branch is one,
With Cullen so young.
Three generations now complete.
The children will be clean, the little girls in new dresses
With petals around the hems, the boys in crisply ironed shirts.

Ring bearer, flower girls, witnesses.
Impressed by our own finery,
We will look toward the camera
That clicks and whirs, hiding the photographer's face.

Great-great-grandchildren will study that photograph,
As naturalists study leaves and petals
Of a flowering tree.
What is the story of these people's lives?
Do I share one's smile, another's eyes,
His humor or her compass-needle sense of direction?

Finding the old photo in a box,
A future child places her sticky finger on Cullen's face,
Saying, "Oh look, there's Granddad as a baby.
He still looks like that when he's grumpy. Has he always been bald?"
She runs to sit on the old man's lap,
And they laugh together at the idea
Of Granddad ever being young.

Bas, Michelle, Gabriel, Pete, Cullen
Robin, Peter, Paul, Laura, Elijah, Paisley
Casey, Reed, Aengus, Maeve
Toronto, 2015

Our New Puppy, or Why I Am Going to Hell

Over the past two months, I watch my gradual descent from a kindly old woman into a dangerous lunatic. I blame the puppy.

At the end of November, 2015, Paul's 70th birthday is coming up, and I want to give him a new laptop. He wants a puppy. He finds a Labradoodle kennel online, buys a puppy, names her Remy, travels to Oregon to pick her up, and brings the eight-week-old home on the first day of December. All goes well for the first few days. Our two nine-year-old Standard Poodles, Corbeau, the black one, and Pegasus, gray, greet the puppy with courteous reserve. Occasionally, they look at me over Remy's head, their eyebrows signaling, "Why?" But that is usually because she is biting their ankles. The cat, Tommy, is appalled and leaves home for three days.

At 1 AM on December 4th, Corbeau starts having violent seizures. He must have been sleeping on the large ottoman that we have near our bed, because I wake to the thump he makes as he falls to the floor. Paul and I turn on the lights. I hold Corbeau's stiffly jerking form in my arms as he has seizure after seizure. Pegasus watches from our bed, and Remy thinks this is a new game that requires pouncing on Corbeau's head.

When I can stand it no longer, I lock Pegasus and Remy in the kitchen: Remy to get her away, and Peggy to keep Remy company.

Paul and I think that the slight pause between each seizure signals the beginning of a return to consciousness, but it never does. Spasms follow each other relentlessly, changing only the muscle groups they choose to contract.

We call the vet. The answering service tells us to take Corbeau to VetMed, the big emergency animal hospital north of the city. Now the question is how to get the seventy-three pound dog into the car. We call the neighbor across the street, but unsurprisingly he doesn't pick up his phone so early on a Sunday morning. Paul manages to slide Corbeau's unconscious body onto a blanket.

I let Pegasus and Remy in to say goodbye. As soon as I open the kitchen door, Pegasus runs to the bedroom, but when she rounds the corner and can see her lifetime partner still lying on the floor, she stops in her tracks and lies down, not approaching the last yard.

Pegasus and Corbeau have never been separated for a minute in the eight years they have lived together. Either from sight or sound or smell, Peggy knows he is almost gone.

Apparently, the smell of terminal illness and the approach of death are not universally recognized by dogs, however. Remy is too young to understand, and continues to play her head-pouncing game.

We half slide/half carry Corbeau in his blanket hammock down the hall and into the car. The seizures are slowing, but he isn't conscious. I shut the other dogs back in the kitchen. Without speaking, we drive through the gray of early morning.

I think everyone except Remy knows how this story will end. In spite of anticonvulsants, Corbeau keeps having seizures all day and never regains consciousness. The emergency vet and our own vet consult and decide that the brain damage is beyond all hope of healing. Paul and I go back to the hospital to say goodbye, sitting beside Corbeau's unconscious form on the floor, telling him that we love him, and reminding him of the dogs he has known who have gone on before, and who will greet him in heaven. Then we nod to the waiting vet.

She puts the final drug in his IV. We watch Corbeau's breathing slow and stop.

We leave the hospital carrying his collar.

On the drive home, Paul and I go over all our favorite stories about Corbeau's exploits. The time as a puppy when he ran past us as we were watching TV, with the end of the toilet paper in his mouth, unrolling the whole spool. How pleased he was when he learned how to open the kitchen door all by himself both from the inside and the outside. His safe-cracking talent of opening the tall garbage drawer and helping himself to its contents, always sharing with a waiting Pegasus. His ability to reach food left anywhere on the kitchen counter. His deep-set brown eyes that looked right into your soul, always finding something of value there. His willingness to lean his head against your hip so you could stroke his curly head. His kindness and courtesy to everyone.

Our plan had been to have two calm, kind dogs to train Remy: to teach her to be housebroken, to open the kitchen door, to walk on a leash, and to steal food from the garbage. But now we are faced with only a severely depressed Pegasus who shows little interest in the unruly Remy, or in life itself. She gets up for breakfast, and then goes back to bed in our room for the rest of the day. As the puppy chews on her ankles, Pegasus looks at us as if to say, "Now I am not only widowed, but I am a single mother to an impossible child." Paul and I sympathize, but there is little we can do about it. We promise to support her through it all, at least financially.

The rest of December is filled with Paul's cataract surgeries. We get a leave of absence from our volunteer job of recording books for the blind at a university library, where I am the reader and Paul is the director. He runs all the computer equipment and listens to my reading, stopping me to correct errors in my pronunciation or pacing. We figure it will take about two weeks for Paul's eyes to heal. First, he has his left eye done, with a new corrective lens implanted where the old clouded cataract had been.

During the week when he is waiting for surgery on his right eye, we walk the dogs around the neighborhood. He opens first his good eye and then his bad one. He is as happy as a pig in mud about the difference. He can see saturated colors and keeps looking at the colors of house paint and saying, "Gray" (right eye), and then, "Actually, bright green" (left eye). Or at the sky, saying, "Gray. Actually, bright blue," And the same with the trees, the asphalt, etc., etc. Naturally, I am happy for him, but I think that commenting on this difference once, or maybe twice, would be sufficient.

Paul has the cataract on his right eye removed, which is a more difficult operation. He says he is more aware and more anxious, and the eight minutes feel like an hour.

A few days after that second cataract operation, Paul notices there is a dark blob in the vision of his right eye. It is now Thursday, Christmas Eve, and the cataract surgery is closed. Paul calls the office and is told that his surgeon is in Colorado but will be back on Sunday and will see him then. Paul is instructed to wait for him. We wait through Christmas and the day after with Bas, Michelle, Elijah, and Paisley, and Paul is very aware of the blob growing bigger until he has vision only in the upper right-hand corner of that eye.

On Sunday, the surgeon takes one look at Paul's eye and sends us to "Retinal Consultants," where the surgeon on call meets us. Paul is scheduled for emergency retinal reattachment surgery on Monday.

I call the recording studio again to update Maria, the woman in charge, and tell her we will need another two weeks off, because Paul is having emergency surgery for a detached retina and will need time to be able to read again.

Maria fires us. "We won't need you anymore," she says. "There won't be enough time for you to finish the book you're working on. I'll give it to someone else."

I don't want to lose this job. "Can we record more often once Paul has healed, in order to make up for the lost time?" I ask her. "Or are there shorter projects we can do?"

She says, "No," to both.

She doesn't seem to notice the irony of firing volunteers who read for the blind for becoming temporarily vision impaired.

I turn my attention back to Paul, who is stressed about this surgery. If the second cataract surgery had made eight minutes seem like sixty, what will a sixty-minute surgery seem like? In addition to asking for every anesthetic drug available, he plans to beg the anesthesiologist to be allowed to take his iPhone into surgery. He has created a playlist to listen to. He also creates a mental playlist in case the iPhone isn't allowed.

It is allowed, but stops playing after the first song. And he isn't allowed to move around to reset it. So he plays his mental playlist instead. It all goes much better than he had anticipated, perhaps proving that pessimism is a strong defense against the unknowable.

The retinal surgeon puts a gas bubble in Paul's eye to support the reattached retina, and Paul spends many days following the doctor's order to sleep on his stomach or his left side to help it along. I administer his drops three times a day, five minutes apart, and Paul describes the vision in his right eye as blurred and like "having a permanent cat toy" in front of him. The slowly shrinking gas bubble bobbles in his line of vision as he walks. Paul can't drive or read or watch TV without a headache. His worry is constant, though he is remarkably stoic about it.

I would like to tell you that I am gentle and sympathetic, but my patience appears to have a shelf life of three days. Since I lived through it with him and know all about it, he has to tell his friends at length about his ordeal. His detailed explanations of his eye surgery single-handedly persuade at least a dozen people never to have their cataracts removed.

I may be impatient, but I'm not stupid. I still have enough sense not to snarl "Not again" at my wounded husband. He looks more vulnerable without his glasses. I smile softly and try to look like a nice person.

Meanwhile, the relentlessly cheerful puppy, Remy, is bouncing all over the house. We hope that her constant teasing of Pegasus will distract the older dog from her grief. Our house is filled with a blur of brown curly fur, moving like an electric dynamo. She is followed by our shouts of "No!" and the smell of poop.

Each morning begins with Remy bouncing around on our faces, pulling at our fingers and ears with needle-sharp teeth to get us up. I understand that crating the puppy would eliminate this problem, but we like sleeping with dogs. Besides, when she is asleep is the only time this puppy is cuddly.

The day begins with cries of:

No Remy, don't steal my slippers,
No, don't bite my ankles.
No, don't bite Pegasus.
No, don't swing from Peggy's ear.
No, don't poop in the front hall.
No, don't swim in your water bowl.
No, don't pull my pajama bottoms down.

And the day proceeds with cries of:

No, Remy, don't dig up Paul's tulip bulbs.
No, don't eat the bare branches of the hibiscus bush.
No, don't unzip your dog bed and pull out the
chopped foam … again.
No, don't put your paw in Peggy's eye.
No, don't put your paw in Paul's eye.
No, don't chew the electric wires.
No, don't climb into the dishwasher to lick the plates.

There are good parts of the day as well. Paul teaches Remy to come when she is called—more often than not. Our granddaughter Paisley, here with her family for Christmas, teaches Remy to sit on command.

Paul takes the two dogs for long walks every day. While he and Peggy come home tired, Remy has a rejuvenating nap in the car on the way back from the desert and is ready to go again. She is now eleven weeks old.

December 31st is the last day of my part-time job, the remaining vestige of my professional life: providing clinical supervision and therapist training in the evidence-based model of Functional Family Therapy. I only partly regret this planned retirement, but unfortunately it frees up more time to realize how angry I am that we were fired from our volunteer job. We have worked there for four years and recorded eight books, coming as often as we are needed. We have never missed a deadline. I rehearse what I will say to Maria when I return her copy of the book we had been recording.

As I enter the small, sunny studio, poor naïve Maria rises from her desk with a smile.

I am feeling wild inside, hot and metallic. I wouldn't be surprised if I give off the scent of blood.

Anger makes my vision clear. All the details of the room stand out in sharp relief. I notice each dust mote suspended in the air by the light from the window. I am held together by a veneer of civilization, no thicker than a coat of paint. I breathe slowly to calm my voice.

I begin the speech I have been practicing. "I would hate for you to think, Maria, even for a moment, that you handled Paul and me at all well. You didn't."

The smile slides slowly from Maria's face.

I put the book in her hand and say, "I am angry at you. You hurt my feelings." Into the pause that follows, I say, "Tomorrow is January first. Possibly you will treat people better next year."

I turn toward the door to leave, and Maria calls after me, "You mustn't take it personally."

I don't have an answer to that. I look back at her with astonishment. I hope that my face expresses my opinion that getting fired is always personal, because I have run out of words for her.

Critical events don't seem done with us yet. On Monday the 4th of January, our dog Peggy seems to slow down. She doesn't wander away from Paul on their walk, even though she isn't leashed. She stays right by his heels with her head down. On Tuesday morning when I call her to come for breakfast, she can barely get off the sofa. She doesn't eat or drink.

At least she hasn't picked a national holiday for this emergency. Our vet has an opening at 9:30. When her blood work comes back with a high white cell count, he sends us back to VetMed for imaging.

Weren't we just here a month ago, saying goodbye to Corbeau?

The vet tech leads Peggy to the back room. Peggy insists on holding her own leash, for comfort. Once again we make ourselves coffee at their Keurig machine in the lobby and take a chocolate from their candy bowl. I am frightened and need caffeine and sugar. We wait in the lobby, watching game shows on the TV and reading old *Arizona Highways*.

The medical imaging shows there is a problem with her gall bladder and another with her spleen, so they schedule surgery for Thursday and send her home with us. However, both our own vet and the vet tech at the hospital tell us to get back in contact quickly if she goes downhill, as the gall bladder can rupture.

By evening, Pegasus has not moved from the corner of the kitchen where she had first lain down. It is time to give her her pills, but she won't eat, drink, or stand up, so Paul props her in a sitting position and I force them down her throat.

It is a great relief to have Paul to talk things over with.

"If these aren't the symptoms of a dog going downhill, I don't know what would be," he says.

We feel quite sure that if we don't do something, we will wake up in the morning to find her dead on the kitchen floor. So we call the vet hospital, and tell them we are on our way back, want her hospitalized overnight, and to get the first surgical appointment possible. We count the blessing that we can afford all this. Peggy can't walk, so we maneuver her onto a large foam dog bed and half drag/half carry her out to the car. We lock the whimpering Remy into the kitchen alone.

We're getting good at this. We don't even bother to call the neighbor for help.

The emergency hospital has other dogs in even less stable shape, so we settle down to wait. One puppy has gotten into a goat pen. I spend a good many minutes trying to figure out what the goats could have done to him, as he doesn't seem at all well.

Another small dog is carried in his human's arms. She announces that he has eaten a packet of dark chocolate. When they take her dog from her, she comes and sits beside me, tearfully explaining that this is the second time he has done this. She tells me with a fierce determination that from now on she is going to put her chocolate in a really thick Tupperware container.

Silently, I rehearse all the ways I can think of to tell this woman she is an utter fool, that Tupperware is an incentive not an obstacle. It indicates the location of buried treasure as surely as an X marked on a canine pirate map. I want to tell her that if she'd stop bringing chocolate home, she wouldn't have this problem, and I wouldn't be waiting in line behind her to have Peggy admitted to the hospital. It seems unsporting of me to lecture her when she is sobbing, so I literally put my hand to my mouth to keep the words in. I hope this can be mistaken for a gesture of concern.

Hours pass. It is the middle of the night, and Paul and I drag Peggy's big dog bed from the car and lie down on it with her in the lobby. We are tired and hope to look so pathetic that we will eventually be given a turn. Finally, they call us. We watch an apathetic Peggy walk with the tech through the swinging doors, once again holding her own leash. We drive home through the dark and arrive in the small, cold hours of the morning.

The vets have agreed to move her surgery ahead and will take out her gall bladder and spleen the next morning.

On Wednesday afternoon, when we are allowed to visit her, she has a stapled incision from her "guggle to her zatch." We lie with her on the floor of the examination room, patting and talking to her until the vet tech returns to say it is time for her next treatment. We can come back tomorrow, she says.

The gall bladder had been badly infected, and there had been a mysterious growth on her spleen and nodules on her liver, all sent off to various pathology labs for identification. There seems to be limited hope.

I want to be told we can bring her home soon, but how am I going to keep Remy off her? The vet asks us if Peggy has ever been away from us before, as she seems depressed.

"She's been away from us lots of times in her life," I reply, "but never from our other poodle, Corbeau, who died last month." Tears run down my face.

I still carry Corbeau's collar in the cup holder of my car. I'm not ready to retire it yet to the basket in the kitchen cupboard that holds a linked chain of seven other dog collars.

We can't bring Peggy home yet. Paul and I bring in the crate we have stored in the garage, from some previous dog's emergency. We set it up in the kitchen and fill its floor with a dog bed. "You must keep her confined," the vet tells us. "She mustn't jump or run."

The next day, we return to VetMed to pay the bill and pick up Peggy. We guide her in and then out of the car by means of a ramp, and bring her into a house that overflows with a wildly dancing puppy. Peggy enters the waiting crate gratefully. We bring her out every two hours for a drink and a short walk to the backyard to pee, but all the time we must fend off the puppy who jumps at her head to make her play.

Every evening, we take Peggy out of the crate so we can carry it, Paul and I at each end, out the wide kitchen door, through the night-filled backyard, and in through the French doors of our bedroom, so that Peggy can sleep near us without being tempted to jump onto our bed. After each brief sortie, she enters her crate again with a sigh of relief.

You would be mistaken to believe that Paul and I are acting as a well-oiled machine all this time, just because I can't write about everything that is going on all at once. The trip from the kitchen to the bedroom, for example, carrying the crate, is typically filled with bickering.

"Watch out, you're going to knock your end against the door frame."

"You've chipped the paint again. It's as if you just don't care."

"Shit, I think I just stepped in shit."

Eventually, it occurs to us to ask around among our dog-owning friends to borrow a second crate so one can stay permanently set up in the bedroom. We continue the intimacy of our bickering as we try to assemble it from unlabeled parts, minus the long-lost instructions.

"You've got your piece upside down."

"Don't be silly, you're just unwilling to turn your part over."

Finally, it is done, we pad its floor with towels, and Peggy moves in with a sigh. Remy can't reach her now and has to content herself with chewing on the thick wire of the crate's walls.

Paul and I make every effort to praise Remy and tell her she is loved. It is sometimes difficult to find something to praise, so we often wake her from a sound sleep and congratulate her on sleeping.

In the mornings, I open the door of the crate, and, fending off the puppy, lead Pegasus, my great, smoke-colored poodle, slowly out into the pearl and pewter-colored dawn. It would be lovely if we weren't being pursued. Remy's onslaught is ceaseless. If she isn't biting Peggy's ankles, she is biting mine. Peggy and I both stop moving every few steps. I say, "No bite," and wait for Remy to release her grip. Then we move another few steps.

I don't believe that Remy is oblivious to the moods of pain and sorrow that surround her in our house.

I may be going slightly mad, but I begin to see Remy as the god Pan, half-human, half-goat: a badly behaved incarnation of the life force. Not life in its gentler aspects, like springtime turning the trees a soft green, but life in all its wild and fierce determination, like a storm at sea.

Remy has a puppy's limited ability to fight back against grief. She is doing her best to distract us and to fill our house with life again. It is as though she would rather see us irritated than sad, even if it means that she is constantly in trouble.

Then, on the other hand, she may just be oblivious.

Gradually, Peggy and I make it to the kitchen with Remy hanging on her ear leather, releasing it only to take great bites of Peggy's nappy coat. I feed them both, then lead Peggy back toward the bedroom to be with Paul.

When I shut the louvered doors to keep Remy in the kitchen, she waits for a second and then bursts through them with great force, lunging for Peggy's ear.

Something inside me stretches to the breaking point and snaps. I stick my foot out to stop her. That may sound civilized, but it isn't. It is accompanied by my thunderous roar of "NO!"

The puppy leaves my foot as a projectile, heading back the way she has come.

It is definitely a kick. I will burn in hell.

Remy gives a series of high-pitched puppy yelps, Peggy looks at me with pity and reproach, Paul comes to see what on earth is going on, and I kneel to apologize to Remy. I would like this to be our secret, but there is no hope of that.

I feel terrible, but at the same time resentful. Not only am I stressed, but I'm turning into a harridan. I have no excuse. I'm well aware that I'm not the one dead of epilepsy, or having emergency eye surgery, or enduring major gall bladder and spleen surgery. I am hale, hearty, impatient, and whiny. I am turning into someone I don't like.

Peggy's health improves for several days and then starts to go downhill again.

I wake one night, and even without my hearing aids I can make out the sound of her vomiting in her crate. I wade through Remy's joy at seeing me up in the middle of the night and open the crate, changing Peggy's bedding while she goes outside to throw up some more.

The next day we take Peggy back to the hospital for more imaging and more blood work. The pathology reports have turned out well: she doesn't have pancreatitis, the growth on the spleen is not cancer, the dangerous gall bladder is gone, and only one of the nodules on the liver seems pre-cancerous. However, the bile duct is inflamed, and the infection is not under control. Like a forest fire, it is only twenty per cent contained. The internist and the surgeon say not to worry about the pre-cancer, they think they got it all. They just hope she'll survive her post-operative recovery.

Peggy comes home that evening with nine medications, some of which must be given with food and others on an empty stomach. Paul and I make spread sheets, fill divided pill boxes, and put Peggy back in her crate.

Remy stands by, her eyes bright and her tongue lolling, cheering us on, a stark contrast to Peggy, who gives the expression "sick as a dog" a sharp new meaning.

Peggy's back where she was a week ago, head hanging, eyes glazed with pain. However, there is a difference. She sometimes lets a sleepy Remy come into her crate, and they lie close together for comfort.

As the days pass, the painkillers, the anti-inflammatories, the antibiotics, the anti-nausea pills, the appetite stimulants, and the liver boosters do their work, and Peggy begins to come back to life.

Remy is relentless, never missing an opportunity to bite Peggy's ankles or swing from her ears. The life force can be damnably painful, like fingers thawing after frostbite. But now Peggy is beginning to take charge. She can tolerate much more than I can, but when she has had enough she turns calmly and snaps at the air a mere millimeter from Remy's nose. Paul and I praise her. When Peggy barks at strangers who come to our gate, Remy hides behind her, memorizing her every canine move for a later time when she, too, will have adult responsibilities.

I used to think of myself as a person with some maturity and self-control. If asked, I might have described myself as patient. All my life I have accepted these comfortable, self-congratulatory lies as truth. However, like Paul from his cataract surgery, I see more clearly now. Life with a puppy in times of stress will do that for a person. Remy tears away the veils of self-delusion with her puppy teeth.

Now I congratulate myself on my insight and humility.

Pegasus and Remy, Phoenix, 2016

Corbeau and Pegasus, Hyannis Port, 2014

Mailing Mother

I mean no disrespect by this essay. I have ambivalent feelings toward my mother, but I'm not ambivalent about respect. I admired her acceptance of the inconveniences and irritations of extreme old age. I hope someday to have her fortitude in the face of loss and her courage in the face of pain. On the other hand, I hope never to be as pig-headed as she was, or as snobbish, or as tactless.

When death comes, even to a woman of ninety-five, it is stressful. Stress, for better or for worse, illuminates the absurdities of life, and makes me laugh.

Jane and I sat in our mother's bedroom for four days in November 2006 listening to her breathe. She never spoke or opened her eyes. We stayed close and talked softly, so she would know we were there.

Jane had tickets to leave Phoenix for her home in Toronto on Sunday. On Saturday night, she and I went out for dinner, leaving mother with her nurse. I burst into tears over my hamburger, begging her to stay. I wasn't sure I'd know what to do on my own.

Jane said, "Well, I can change my flight to Monday, but that's the absolute longest I can stay. I have to get home."

Mother was cooperative and died on Sunday night.

Jane left Monday morning, having helped me choose a mortuary, and they guided me through the forms and signatures. You'd think that with Mother safely dispatched to heaven, the stressful parts would be over, but you'd be wrong. Now a new set of stressors began.

First came my arrangements with the mortuary—all very straightforward. Mother had wanted her body cremated and the ashes buried in the old family cemetery in Ramapo, New York. The mortuary said they would hold the ashes as long as I needed, until I could make burial arrangements.

Next came the visit from the social worker from hospice. I was in Mother's apartment, sorting through her things and making piles of what to give away, what to throw out, and what to send to relatives, when the doorbell rang. A stranger stood there, a rather wild-eyed woman, with a cloud of unruly hair and a look of determination. "Hello, I'm the grief counselor from hospice, here to help you."

It seemed disrespectful to Mother to say that I wasn't grieving. So

I let her in and we sat in the study. I was grateful to stop my sorting for a few minutes.

I tried to explain that my mother had been ninety-five, and that I was sixty, that this death had hardly been a case of premature abandonment.

The social worker insisted. "Well dear, you may not feel it now, but it will hit you later, so we should set up a series of sessions."

"No," I said, "we shouldn't. But you can help me with the sorting if you'd like."

We had quite a tussle over whether I was grieving or not, and although I never convinced her, I did eventually get rid of her.

A month or two passed with me working every weekend on cleaning out Mother's apartment.

The mortuary called me occasionally, never pressuring, just wanting to remind me they still had Mother. It was time to get her ashes to New York. I called Jack, a New York relative, and he said sure, he'd hold onto the ashes if I sent them, waiting until the ground thawed and Jane and I could bury her. "But how do I send them?" I asked.

"Oh, just mail them at the post office," Jack replied.

I picked up the ashes at the mortuary. They were in a nice little cardboard box. Mother had given a lot of thought to how she was going to be buried. She'd had two husbands and had decided to be buried next to Richard, my father, along with a few spoonfuls of her second husband's ashes mixed with hers, the rest of Sam buried with his previous wife, Ellie.

I'd had that packet of Sam's ashes kicking around my house for the nine years since his death, but where was it now? I searched everywhere, drawers, closets, mantle pieces, all the normal places you'd put a small packet of ashes labeled "Sam."

Finally, when I was just about to give up and bury Mother without a bit of Sam, earning her eternal displeasure, I found him. He was on one of the bookshelves in the living room.

I opened Mother's cardboard box, added Sam, then re-taped it.

My greatest concern was that the USPS might not mail cremains. If not, then what? I didn't want to fly with her under my arm, as I thought the box might alarm security, and I didn't want her confiscated.

I put Mother's box in a larger cardboard box, carefully addressed to Jack, and stood in line at the Post Office, balancing Mother on my hip.

The postmistress looked at my box and asked the regulation questions, "Does this contain anything potentially hazardous? Flammable, liquid, explosive?"

I said no to each item. Perhaps I looked guilty, because she wasn't satisfied with my answers. She looked me in the eye, and said, "Well, what is in it then?"

Rats, I thought. I came up with a stuttered, "It's a memorial object."

"What kind of memorial object?" she pursued relentlessly.

"My mother's ashes," I said, capitulating, and waited to be told to take it home.

"Hmmm," the postmistress intoned, giving my box a sharp glance. "I'll have to tape it again."

With that, she proceeded to tape every inch of that box, seams and surfaces. Mother wasn't going to slip out anytime soon.

I was startled by her thoroughness, wondering whether she thought ashes contain germs and that death was contagious. But I was too grateful she was going to mail it to ask her.

When she had finished, and the box was now nearly round with tape, she looked at me and said, "Please accept my condolences on the loss of your mother."

That was kind, I thought. Perhaps tape was her form of respect.

I thanked her for her courtesy and was turning away when I saw her toss the box over her shoulder, across the aisle and into the canvas-sided bin of outgoing mail.

Nevertheless, Mother had a safe trip, and I heard a few days later that she had arrived safely and was sitting in a corner of Jack's office.

By April, the ground was soft and the grass was green. Jane and I met in New York and drove out to Ramapo together. We joined Jack, who brought Mother's box to the cemetery.

It was just the three of us, Jane, Jack, and me, at the burial. It's a small cemetery but tidy because a custodian was doing a spring cleanup of old leaves. His wife is buried there, and he likes to keep it neat. He'd dug a narrow hole with a posthole digger in front of the new tombstone we'd had erected for Mother. He said hello and then withdrew a discreet distance. Jack went with him.

The tombstone had all the information Mother had directed us to put on it. Mother always thought people should have informative tombstones for the convenience of future genealogists.

The hole seemed a bit deep. I couldn't see the bottom of it. I suggested that Jane, as the eldest, might want to lower Mother into the hole, but she said, as the eldest, she didn't think she could get far enough down onto the ground.

"All right," I said, stooping gracefully. There was no way I could stoop low enough. I knelt on the damp spring earth, and leaned forward. I still couldn't lower Mother into that hole with anything like dignity.

I squirmed myself into a prone position, my cheek pressed against the damp grass, and extended one arm, holding the box as far as it would reach down that hole. Still unable to feel the bottom, I dropped Mother the last twelve inches.

Jane, Jack, and the custodian were too far away to hear the thud, or my words, "Bye, Mom. Sorry about that."

Jane pulled me back up on my feet, and we all went out to lunch.

Possibly Could Be Read as a Eulogy

When Paul and I retired, we decided we'd spend the summer months in my childhood home on Cape Cod. We had inherited this house from my parents, but as we live 3,000 miles away, we have rented it out for the last thirty years in order to be able to keep it.

It's a strange feeling, returning to a house you knew well as a child but haven't lived in for decades. The house is the same, the town is the same, the ocean is the same, but I am different. I can no longer jump out of bed in the morning and run downstairs to eat breakfast with my parents. I can no longer run barefoot across the gravel driveway, as the ratio of my foot surface to body weight has changed in a painful and alarming way. I can no longer be outside in all weathers with a bit of Noxzema on my nose. The adults I knew as a child are dead now, and the children I grew up with have become old in their turn. Paul and I have the basic survival and safety needs taken care of, but how do we forge a sense of belonging in a new place?

Maslow's Hierarchy puts "a sense of belonging" about halfway up his graphic depiction of a pyramid of human needs. At the bottom are air, water, food, shelter—all the necessities for survival. Above that is the need for security and safety. Then comes "Belonging," and above it is "Esteem"—a need for prestige and a sense of accomplishment—and, finally, the small wedge at the top of the pyramid, "Self-Actualization," the need for creativity and fulfilling one's potential.

The way I translate Maslow's understanding of human motivation is that once we're warm, fed, and safe, we will immediately look around for a way to belong to some kind of pack, whether friends or family doesn't really matter, and then look for ways to elevate our status and prestige in order to rise to the top of that pack. We are really not satisfied until our pack unanimously declares that we are so wonderful that we belong in another pack entirely: perhaps with Noble Peace Prize winners, or the Catholic hagiography of saints. We humans are not only transparent in our ambitions, but also predictable.

Paul and I fill the house and our summers with our kids and grandkids. They are all happy to have a few days at the beach. We invite friends from Phoenix to come as well, but we realize that if we are going to continue to live in Hyannis Port every summer for the foreseeable future, we have to make a life for ourselves here. Two by two, we invite the neighbors over for drinks on the porch. And the ones we like get invited back for dinner. We are invited to their houses for drinks and dinners. It is a very slow and tedious process, and requires a facility for light conversation that I don't have and don't want to develop.

Last summer, in an effort to speed up our socializing, Paul and I decided to look into joining the local golf club. I called and asked for membership services.

"Hello," I said. "My husband and I are interested in joining the club and would like to find out how to go about it."

"Well," said a woman's dubious voice at the other end of the line, "it's not easy. You understand that you would have to be sponsored by one member, and then obtain letters of reference from three others. Do you know four people who are currently members?"

"Yes," I countered, "I understand your club is charmingly exclusive, and naturally you wouldn't want to let anyone in who didn't already know all your other members. But assuming, just for the moment, that I can bribe four of your current members to vouch for me, what would a membership cost?" I grabbed a pen and a pad of paper, ready to take notes.

The woman seemed disappointed that I didn't want to continue to explore the humiliation of not already being a member, but she reluctantly moved on.

"The couple's initiation fee for you and your husband would be $50,000, and then there would be the annual dues of $5,000, plus the food allowance for the restaurant. That's $700 a year, for the four months that our club is open, which you forfeit if you don't spend it all. And of course this doesn't include greens fees for the golf course or the cost of playing tennis."

I scribbled all these numbers down, while Paul looked at them over my shoulder.

"So, as I understand it," I said, "that $50,000 allows us to stand in your vestibule, and makes honest people of us when we take our dogs for a walk on your golf course every evening?"

"You do what?"

Moving along quickly, I said, "That seems kind of high considering my husband and I are seventy and won't have many years left to enjoy your lovely club. Do you pro-rate that initiation fee for senior citizens?"

"No."

"Do you have social memberships, if we promise never to play golf or tennis?"

"No."

I tore the top page off my pad, screwed it into a ball, and aimed it across the room. It fell to the floor at my feet.

"Do you actually have anybody who wants to join your club?" I asked.

At this point my husband removed the phone from my hand and gently hung it up.

"Well," I announced, "I'm not spending my grandchildren's college fund on membership to a group reliving the 1950s. I dislike golf, I was never any good at tennis, the club restaurant has linen tablecloths and makes all the small boys dress in coats and ties. I didn't like the 1950s on my first time through, and I see no reason to do them twice."

"Yes, yes," he said soothingly.

For a reason I cannot fathom, people often try to soothe me.

"Well," continued Paul, "we could always buy plots for ourselves at Mt. Auburn Cemetery instead."

That may sound like a non-sequitur, but not if you think about it in terms of Maslow's Hierarchy. It's an idea that combines every level of human need. It meets the basic survival needs, just a bit differently, that's all. We won't need air and food and water, but we'll still need a space and a roof over our ashes.

Then there's safety and security—what could be more secure than a spot six feet underground?

Moving on to "Belonging" and then "Esteem," we would be in with the most illustrious people of eighteenth-, nineteenth-, and twentieth-century America. Now, that's an exclusive group: Winslow Homer, Henry Wadsworth Longfellow, Louis Agassiz, Mary Baker Eddy, Nathaniel Bowditch, and Benjamin Hallowell, to name a few. And the prestige!

When future generations come to visit us, they may think we belong there, not realizing that anyone can buy a plot.

I felt self-actualized just thinking about it.

And there will be other benefits. I won't have to play golf and tennis. There will be no annual restaurant charges. The membership fee is a fraction of the price of the club, and can be paid in installments. Membership will begin, rather than end, at our deaths.

Buried in a beautiful garden, Paul and I will wander the grounds late at night, after the groundskeepers have gone home for the day, and have deep conversations with some of the most interesting people in earth.

A Deep Conversation with an Interesting Person

When I have trouble falling asleep, I lie in bed staring at the ceiling and tell myself stories. This one explores the question, "If I could talk to anyone alive or dead, who would it be?"

*　　　*　　　*　　　*

First, I become aware of my feet, moving one in front of the other along a well-traveled dirt road. The dust of the road is so light that it is almost white. A thin layer of it collects on the toes of my well-polished boots as each step brings first one and then the other out from under the hem of my long black dress. As the dust hits the hem, I watch the bottom six inches turn slowly gray.

There is no past and no future. I am simply here. I might believe that I have lost my memory, except I know that a few minutes ago, at the beginning of this experience, my boots and hem were clean.

Where am I, and why am I here? I look up from my feet and see the dry country on either side. It is a warm winter day, pale brown and gray, with an occasional tree casting thin shade on the road. A flock of sheep grazes on the hillside. There are no automobiles, and no sound of planes overhead. The air tastes of dust and dry leaves, with no metallic aftertaste. I hold a warm wool shawl around my shoulders, and I am dressed from neck to ankles in a full-skirted black dress. The word that comes to my mind is bombazine. I have no idea what bombazine is. I add a new question to my list: When am I?

The only thing I know is that I am me. It surprises me that I have no anxiety, only curiosity.

As I walk along, the trees become more closely set, and the pattern of their shade on the road more regular. Ahead of me, with single-point perspective, I can see the dirt road narrowing and ending at high iron gates set in a long stone wall, and beyond the wall the roof of a large building. I walk close enough to read the wooden sign set in the wall to the left of the gate: "L'Hôpital—Arles."

First shaking some of the dust off my hem, I sit on a bench by the gate to think. I note that in the absence of anxiety comes a sharper-than-usual clarity.

Unlikely as the answers to "where" and "when" seem, they are also fairly simple. Arles tells me I am in southern France, and my dress suggests the third quarter of the nineteenth century. That leaves the "why." As I stare at the blank, uncommunicative wall on my right, I realize there is only one way in which the where and the when intersect. This is Vincent van Gogh's world.

One answer to the "why" question would be that I am here to talk to Vincent, so I'd better figure out how to do that. I can see that the gate is locked, with a cord attached to a bell to summon an attendant. But what can I say that will get me in? All right, I'll say I'm Vincent's sister, Wilhelmina, come from Holland to visit him. I can only hope that Vincent will be either too delusional to notice that I'm not Wilhelmina, or that he will be sane enough to go along with this lie. I sincerely hope that he is not just on the cusp of sanity and that my claim to be Wilhelmina pushes him over the edge again.

I rise from the bench and pull the cord. A distant bell rings. Through the wrought-iron gate, I watch a nun in a dark blue habit, white apron and wimple, approach across the courtyard. She looks at me questioningly. I open my mouth, wondering what will come out of it.

My rusty French suddenly becomes fluent, with a slight Dutch accent. "I am Wilhelmina van Gogh," I say, as imperiously as possible. "I've come to see my brother Vincent."

"Follow me," says the little nun softly. "I will let Dr. Rey know that you have arrived. He received your letter last week and has been expecting you."

I follow her across the porticoed courtyard, past the central fountain and the dormant flower beds.

She indicates a bench for me while she knocks on a door marked "Felix Rey, Docteur de Médecin."

The good doctor opens his door, and the nun introduces us. Dr. Rey greets me with a smile and takes my hand as I rise from my seat. "Ah, Mademoiselle van Gogh, this is a sad reunion for you, I know. But your brother is receiving the best of care."

"Please, may I go to him?" I ask hurriedly, hoping to forestall any questions about my journey.

"Of course, of course," the doctor replies, taking my arm at the elbow and leading me up a flight of broad stone stairs. "I am afraid that your brother's appearance may shock you. His ear is healing well, but he is sadly underweight and is often agitated. You will, I know, take his appearance calmly and not upset him."

"Of course," I say. I still feel no anxiety, but neither am I confident that I will do this right.

Dr. Rey leads me to a large dormitory room, with a pot-bellied stove in the middle and sad, silent figures seated around it. Curtained alcoves, each with a bed in it, line the long sides of the room. He pulls aside one curtain to reveal a thin, red-headed man asleep in his clothes on a narrow bed.

"Vincent," he shouts jovially, "wake up, man! I've brought your dear sister to visit you."

I wonder just how dear Wilhelmina is to Vincent. I hope for the best.

Vincent opens his eyes and regards me solemnly, showing neither surprise nor alarm.

As I had hoped, he keeps his mouth shut, and I find myself gabbling. "Ah, dear brother, it is I, Wilhelmina, come to visit you." While Doctor Rey goes to fetch me a chair, I lean toward Vincent and whisper, "Don't give me away. I'll explain everything later."

Vincent doesn't seem agitated by my sudden appearance, and he slowly swings his legs over the side of his bed and sits up. There are holes in his socks. His sheets are gray. His bed looks like a nest. I long to strip his tumbled sheets and wash them. What are the nuns doing with their time? But I don't believe I've been sent here to wash Vincent's sheets.

I take the chair offered by Dr. Rey, and Vincent and I regard each other levelly, both waiting for the reluctant doctor to leave.

"Ah, yes. Then I'll leave you alone for your reunion," Dr. Rey says, turning to go.

Once we're alone, Vincent says, "Who the hell are you? Are you real?"

As the answer to the first question will tell him nothing, I skip it. "I'm real. You're not imagining me, or at least we are both imagining the same thing. As far as I know, I've been sent from the future to talk to you."

"What about?" he asks, narrowing his eyes in irritation.

"All I know is that my way has been made easy, so I believe I am supposed to talk to you, but I wasn't given a script. Perhaps you have questions I could answer?" I add hopefully.

"You're probably just another nut case," Vincent says unsympathetically, casting a quick glance around the room to see whether there's an empty bed, and a patient unaccounted for.

"Look, Dr. Rey brought me over, so he can see me, too, and he doesn't think I'm a patient. I don't know how long we've got, and I have no idea why it was thought to be a good idea to create an irrational scene for a man who has recently been delusional, but that's what we've got."

"That makes it much clearer," he murmurs with an edge of sarcasm.

A pause follows, neither of us speaking. Then we speak together.

"You look well," I say, just as he says, "You look nothing like Wilhelmina."

We both stop, and he glares at me. "There's not much point in your coming here," he says, "if you're going to mouth platitudes."

"True, you're not looking all that well. You look as though you haven't slept in a month, and—"

"That's better," he interrupts, "although I don't need details." He narrows his eyes again as he considers my face, though whether in irritation or amusement is impossible to tell on such short acquaintance. "So what's the future like?" he asks.

"Filled with machines and new inventions. There are medicines in the future for your mental illness."

"Did you bring them?" he asks, without much interest.

"No," I reply slapping the skirt of my dress, hoping for pockets but finding none.

"Absinthe?" he asks, with more interest.

I pat again. "Still no. I wasn't given anything to bring."

"So much for you being of any practical help then." Vincent half turns from me, and stares across the room. The pause stretches out, then he asks softly, "What is my own future?"

I think for a moment, and somehow I know that telling anyone how much time he has and how he will die is forbidden. Specific information would never be allowed to leave my mouth. "You will paint many more pictures," I offer, finally.

Vincent turns back to look at me and snorts. "You'll have to do better than that," he says. "I paint even when I'm mad. Will I hurt anyone? Can I trust myself if I'm not confined?"

"Yes," I say quickly, "you would never hurt another person." And then I realize from the sharpening of his glance that he has caught the nuance of my statement.

He looks down at his square, workman's hands and says something I cannot hear. I move from my chair to sit beside him on the bed, which requires the arrangement and rearrangement of my long skirt. The whole thing is unorthodox, but no one seems to notice or care.

"When will I sell my pictures?" he repeats.

This I can answer without hesitation. "I can't give you dates, but I can promise you that people will buy every single picture, right down to the smallest, most inconsequential sketch. They will sell for millions and millions of francs."

"So only rich people will see them?"

"No, lots of them will be in museums for everyone to see, and they will be reproduced as prints and copied on clothes, calendars, coffee mugs, and coasters."

He has begun to look interested, and then gets momentarily sidetracked, asking, "What are coasters?"

"Never mind coasters," I say, putting my hand on his sleeve. "You know the painting you did last year of sunflowers?"

He sits still, remembering.

"Well, that picture will be on postage stamps and pill boxes, and every possible surface that will take print."

"God save us, how dreadful," he says, the deepening crease between his brows giving his face a look of pain.

I feel a bit discouraged by his reaction. "No, really, it's not dreadful! It's a bit irritating, yes, but it's only because everyone loves you, and they all want a piece of you."

"You mean my paintings, not me." He looks uncomfortable and stares at my hand where it still rests on his sleeve.

I remove my hand and place it with the other one in my lap.

He continues. "Won't the people of the future know that I am the 'Fou Rouge?' That I am not acceptable?"

"It's not just your paintings, it's you," I continue stubbornly. "And you're not just acceptable, you're loved!" I take a breath and continue more calmly. "Your brother Theo will save not only your paintings but also your letters. They will be published and republished in dozens of languages."

The light from the windows is beginning to fade with the early winter dusk, and for a few minutes we watch in silence as the nuns move quietly around the room lighting the oil lamps. The pools of golden light add color to the room.

"I don't write Theo the whole truth, you know," Vincent says, his voice low and unsure, his deep set eyes now staring directly into mine. "I don't burden him with every hurt and disappointment of my life. It's better for both of us if we focus on our work and ideas."

For a moment I think his statement over, aware of our shoulders touching companionably as we sit on his bed leaning back against the wall. The rough canvas curtains on either side give us a sensation of privacy, and the opening in front lets us look out at the room while we talk.

"You mean you think in the future people won't know all the facts about you?" I ask. "I may have failed to mention the scores of biographies that will be written about you, which will detail both your triumphs and your failures. But for anyone who wants to know you in your own words, there will be your letters.

"Your voice will always accompany your paintings. You talk to us about how you have created wonder and joy out of sorrow. Your courage gives us hope. That is why we love you."

I am surprised when Vincent slowly takes my hand in his. He begins haltingly. "So the present is not all there is? Because in the present, everything I do is wrong. Every step I take is misplaced. I am clumsy and I say the wrong thing. People turn their backs. It hurts. And another thing," he continues without pausing. "I depend on Theo for everything, and he should be saving his money to marry Johanna."

I press my back against the wall and search for the right words. "You may think that supporting you is a burden to Theo, but in fact he needs to support you. It is knowing that you need him that keeps him going."

"He won't give up on me?"

"Never."

We stare down at our linked hands. Vincent speaks quietly. "He's all I have. I love him and he's the only one who loves me back."

My thumb slowly traces the tendons on the back of his hand and I ask, "Do you remember saying once, 'The more I think about it, the more I realize there is nothing more artistic than to love others.'"

For the first time, Vincent looks genuinely amused. "I don't think I have said that yet, but now I will."

I grin at Vincent and squeeze his hand. "I know why I'm here. The future sent me to thank you. Thank you for your courage and your strength. Thank you for showing us the beauty of simple things, and for painting what you see in the colors of joy."

The same gentle nun who opened the gate to me earlier in the day approaches me again. I know she is coming to tell me I must leave.

Quickly, I repeat a stanza that Vincent once wrote to Theo.

O never think the dead are dead,
So long as there are men alive,

The dead will live, the dead will live.*

I smile at the nun, as I rise from Vincent's bed. She doesn't appear surprised. Standing, I look down to smooth my skirt, then raise my face to Vincent's. He sits on his bed, watching me. I reach for his hand, "Goodbye," I say, leaning in to kiss first one bearded cheek, then the other.

Reluctantly, I turn to follow the nun. Like the beginning, when there had been no fear, now there is no grief. I turn at the door for one last look, and Vincent half raises his hand to me in acknowledgment.

Walking back through the garden, to the gate, I am aware that the nun is chattering away to me, but I'm not listening.

I thank her for her hospitality, turning back to the dusty road that brought me here.

I listen to the wind in the bare branches, and even in the winter twilight, I can see that the dust on my boots is getting lighter with each step I take.

---

*Author unknown, quoted by Vincent in a letter to Theo, *The Complete Letters of Vincent Van Gogh,* Vol II (New York: Bullfinch Press, 2008) 538.

Guardians

I.

Crows perch in pines around the house
Raucous and protective.
I live in their territory,
Guarded with their own.

Crows quicken my interest,
And make me smile.
I nod to one in recognition of my bond.
He looks at me, then turns away.

One dawn, the entire murder caws its alarm,
Like a town's cracked bells all striking together,
Wild and abandoned,
Signaling disaster.

Crows gather in the surrounding trees to keen,
Mourning the death of one of their own.
A crow corpse lies at the curve of the dirt road.
When my turn comes, I hope I will be missed like that.

I put hamburger for them under the trees,
In hopes of making friends.
Three young crows come down to eat,
While a larger crow sits on the branch above,
Yelling bloody murder.

"Don't put that in your mouth!" she shouts.
"You don't know where it's been!"
Like children, they ignore her good advice,
Believing themselves immortal.

But they are not persuaded by my gift.
Impressed by her furious concern instead,
They eat, then fly. Not to return today.

Crow friendship can't be bought.

The dogs lie silent in the backyard
While the crows all bark a warning.
I step outside to find the danger
And see a fox standing in my sunlit drive.

"Really, dogs? You notice nothing?"
The fox slips into the underbrush.
The sound of cawing grows more distant
As crows escort her off their land.

II.

In the half-light of a winter afternoon in Paris,
I stand in the park with bread in my hand,
Offering my heart to the crows.
First one, and then another, comes to me.

I toss them pieces
Of bread and admiration.
They pass the word.
From each bare tree they come,
Until I am surrounded.

They push closer until I am riding
A cloud of blue-black iridescence.
They lift me on their wings.
I am a crow until the bread runs out.

Raven, by Laura de Blank, watercolor on paper, 2007

The Quilt

The cutlery drawer of the old Welsh dresser
Is filled with colors instead of spoons.
Pull the drawer, and spools of every shade roll forward,
Like parrots, shouting, "Me, me, me!"

The wide shelves of the Japanese armoire
Once held the soft kimonos
Of ladies and gentlemen of Kyoto,
Now carry folded wools, cottons, and silks.

Plain white flannel stretched upon a frame
Makes a design wall as wide as any bed.
It leans against the bookshelves of the living room,
A backdrop for scraps of cloth, rearranged endlessly.

The sewing machine sits in a corner of the kitchen
Thinking it's invisible under a dust cloth.
When brought to life, a deus ex machina,
It creates order out of chaos, and trips the unwary.

Tools are hidden everywhere: thread, cloth, rulers heaped in
        trembling stacks,
Drawers of cutters and needles, ruled mats tucked behind sofas,
And six seam rippers. Can one ever have enough?
The workroom doubles as a living space.

Bright color, rattling noise, mumbled curses,
An audio book from the library, all
Imbue each quilt with character: courage and honor in equal parts.
Dragon adventures, ghost stories, mysteries.

The quilt will be pieced, sewn, ironed,
Boxed and shipped,
A gift of protection from all cold and damp:
A bed cover, a picnic blanket, a shroud.

219

Now I Lay Me Down to Sleep, quilt by Laura de Blank, cotton, 70" x 90", 2007

President Trump

I am not a political person, which explains why my essays do not include memories of a political nature. However, I can imagine the dismay of my grandchildren and great-grandchildren when they look at the dates covered in my memoirs, turn eagerly to the end to find some mention of the presidential election of 2016, just to find I didn't think it was important enough to mention. It would be like reading a memoir of the 1860s and finding no thoughts on the Civil War.

I am writing this essay on November 15, 2016, just one week after Trump won the presidential election. It is too soon to tell whether we are heading into our own era of Civil War Post-Reconstruction. I think we are. Trump has named Steve Bannon, an Alt Right White Nationalist as his chief strategist and senior advisor. I am sad and ashamed that Bannon will become a powerful voice in America. Trump's win is a victory for white racism.

Trump's speeches have covered a variety of topics. Build a wall along our southern border and make Mexico pay for it. More jobs for the working class through tax breaks for wealthy entrepreneurs, and heavy tariffs on imported goods. Tougher negotiating skills with other countries. Global warming is a hoax. Affordable health care is unaffordable.

But always, underneath the words of his speeches and of his campaign slogan "Make America Great Again," runs the thinly veiled message Make America White Again.

Trump's campaign rallied Americans around fear and hatred. He brought out the worst in my countrymen. He snarled and spat his disdain for women, racial minorities, Muslims, and the disabled. He called the people who disagreed with him "losers." He played upon people's fear of others, suggesting that only in homogeneity lay safety. Trump suggested that if minorities prospered, whites would have less status and privilege, and if the United States was part of a global trading community, there would be fewer jobs and less money for America's workers.

In Germany, they call Trump "America's Hitler." Trump has the same demagoguery, the same ability to inflame, the same desire to scapegoat weaker groups for general social and economic troubles, the same simplistic solutions to complex problems, and the same willingness to see violence as the solution. He has encouraged his followers to attack physically those who disagree with him, thus endangering the right of free speech and peaceful assembly. He has made every one of us less safe in our own land.

Trump's win was a surprise to the population and to the pollsters. Paul and I watched the election coverage on Fox news, the most conservative of the television channels. Even Fox was grave as it showed the nation's map, with state after state going for Trump. There was no jubilation in their announcements. I went to bed before the count was completely finished, too sad to watch. I lay there staring at the ceiling, too troubled to sleep. I admire Paul for staying up and watching it through.

I hoped that the minorities would save the United States from Trump. I couldn't imagine women and people of color voting for him. But enough of them did.

Hillary Clinton won the popular vote by almost 2.9 million people, but Donald Trump won the electoral vote, so he will be president. It is not an exaggeration to say that over half the voting population is in mourning right now. But forty-three per cent of the population did not vote.

The United States has passed through an eight-year period of increasing tolerance. In 2008, the election of Barack Obama, our first African American president, was a milestone. My reaction to Obama's election was very different from my feelings during Trump's. As the television showed Obama's state-by-state election results, my joy increased until I could sit still no longer. When it was clear that Obama had won, I grabbed Paul's hand and pulled him outdoors.

"We are going to dance in the streets," I said. "I want to be able to tell our grandchildren that when America finally united enough to elect an African American president, that you and I were out dancing in the streets."

It was a quiet night, lit by the yellow glow of street lamps and the moon. Paul and I started with a waltz and twirled around on the empty street in front of our house, but with only the music of our own humming, we soon switched to the dances of our youth: the jitterbug, the twist, and a bit of the frug thrown in for good measure. We weren't graceful, but we were filled with joy. Our country was overcoming its centuries of racism.

During Obama's two terms, the spirit of tolerance and inclusion continued. In spite of Congress sabotaging everything Obama stood for, the nation witnessed the recognition of gay and lesbian rights, first given in the military, then spreading state by state until people no longer had to hide who they were and all had the right to marry. We gained universal affordable health care. Obama was elected for a second term.

In 2016, we saw our first female candidate for president nominated by a major political party. Obama spoke with reasoned calm as he negotiated with foreign powers in the global arena. He gained the respect and affection of the world.

My admiration for Barack Obama goes deeper than my factual memory.

In 2010, I had a bout of Transient Global Amnesia, a temporary condition that causes an inability to form new memories and to recall the past. It is as if a switch has been thrown and your mind has to reboot. I was with Paul and Bas when it happened. Paul suddenly realized that I couldn't answer even the simplest question, and fearing I'd had a stroke, he and Bas rushed me to the hospital for a multitude of tests. They sat with me and told me later about the seven hours that I lost. In retrospect, after the crisis had passed, they enjoyed telling me about my conversations with the neurologist who, expecting me to "wake up" at any time, asked me repeatedly, "Who is the President of the United States?"

For hours I didn't know the answer, but each time, when I was told it was Barack Obama, I grinned with delight and said, "Wonderful!"—again and again and again.

Now, in 2016, Trump has put out the call to Americans to undo the past eight years of increasing tolerance in the name of defending the Constitution and traditional values. He has dismissed tolerance, calling it weakness. He has promised to undo women's rights to abortion, LGBTQ rights, the ability of undocumented migrants to find a legal path to citizenship, and the right of healthcare for 20,000,000 people—just about everyone's rights but his own.

I would like to go back out to the street, not to dance this time, but to break windows and burn random buildings in my anguish over what is happening to my country. But that would amount to the violence that Trump condones and encourages. I am constrained by my belief that the foundation of a democracy is the ability of the minority to become the majority without bloodshed. I will find a way to respect the people who voted for Trump, and have a reasoned dialogue with them.

I cannot just hunker down and wait out the storm of Trump's

term, hoping for a better future. I must do something.

I will speak out against racism in all its forms. I pledge to be an ally to those targeted by intolerance. I will fight for the rights of everyone in my country not only to be safe, but to be respected.

President Obama would want me to.

The Gift

Twenty-five feet ahead:
The old beggar sits, cross-legged, on the sidewalk.
Dark buildings tower over him. Workday people step around him.
Traffic flashes by.
He stares at the sidewalk, holding a cardboard sign—
Too small for me to read.

Twenty feet:
I walk closer.
Homeless men sit on benches,
Turning their faces to the weak winter sun.
Dogs sit by their sides.

Fifteen feet:
Pitbulls mostly—well fed, unleashed.
One man rises to leave. His dog, with innocent menace,
Shadows him through the crowded streets.

Ten feet:
The beggar's legs are thin as sticks. A jacket pads his sunken chest.
The cap covering his head hides his face.
He shows his sign to hurrying strangers.
No one stops.

Five feet:
Not looking up, he turns his sign my way.
"Please help me."
I slow my step.

Zero feet:
I walk past him,
This old, gray man who takes so little
Space on the pavement.

Zero minus two feet:
I turn back, reaching for loose dollars in my pocket.

Zero feet:
I put my dollars in his cup.
I turn to go, then pause.
He lifts his face to look at me.
His eyes are the blue of heaven.
His smile takes my breath away.

What Is Important in My Life—Paul

I am afraid of trying and failing to portray a love affair of fifty years. A long, steady affair lacks the pizzazz of a new beginning, or the intensity of an ending. It has had those moments, of course, but is not defined by them. Instead, it is defined by its Rock-of-Gibraltar stability and its feather-mattress comfort—crucial for survival, but lacking in drama.

Paul and I met in the first class of our first semester at Stanford University. We were seventeen years old at the time. We began dating when we were nineteen, and we married at twenty-one.

We have been together three times longer than we have been single. We've traveled through various graduate schools, several bleak Army towns, Paul's stint in Viet Nam, eleven household moves in our first nine years of marriage, three children, two satisfying careers, and seven grandchildren. Simultaneously, nothing much and everything.

Our love had drama at the beginning. There were the chemical portents: the warm silk of his skin, the scent of his neck, the electric touch of his hand on my arm, the glances that met and lingered. Then there were the stumbling advances and retreats. In our junior year when I got strep throat for the third time in two months, and was sent to the school infirmary, I didn't tell Paul where I was, because if he really loved me he would find me. And he did, bringing me chocolate ice cream and sympathy.

After marriage, we found a way to settle comfortably into harness together like two rather attractive oxen pulling the plow of life. We had a job to do together: to make a home for children and for each other, a safe place to return to from the outside world. But we also developed individual interests: our own professional worlds, our separate friendships and hobbies, but always we were pulled back together by our history and by our future.

Paul would introduce me to adventures, some of which worked and others that didn't. For several years, he carried me off, kicking and screaming, to the opera, where I would spend hours counting my teeth with my tongue, always coming up with a different total, and suffering through "restless leg syndrome" caused by boredom and the scratchiness of velvet seats. Finally, he admitted defeat and would

227

invite one of his harem of female friends instead.

And now that the children are grown and gone, with families and children of their own, and we have retired from our jobs, our focus is gently shifting from the tasks we have to do, to each other. Now love is defined differently. Paul still calls me "Lauralove," although usually without noticing what he's said, and just as often in exasperation as in affection.

We bicker on long car drives and have to ask Google to arbitrate. Paul is always right, and I always forgive him for being so. We divide up the work of driving. When stopped at red lights he is in charge of which direction to go, and I'm in charge of the colors: "It's green, Paul.... It's not going to get any greener."

At night, we read in bed together, my head on his chest. And in the morning, when I wake, the first thing I do is stretch my leg out to touch him, to determine if he is still beside me, or has gotten up to make the coffee.

Paul and Laura, 2015